THE TABERNACLE

M. R. DeHAAN, M.D.

Lamplighter Books Grand Rapids, Michigan
Zondervan Publishing House

THE TABERNACLE
Copyright © 1955 by Zondervan Publishing House
Grand Rapids, Michigan

Copyright renewed 1983 by Ruth Haaksma

Lamplighter Books are published by Zondervan
Publishing House, 1415 Lake Drive, S.E.,
Grand Rapids, Michigan 49506

ISBN 0-310-23491-3

Printed in the United States of America

86 87 88 89 90 / 35 34 33 32

CONTENTS

FOREWORD

The messages in this volume were first prepared for radio broadcasts, and were given in a consecutive series over two coast-to-coast networks of radio stations. They appear in this volume essentially as they were delivered over the air, with a minimum of editing or alteration. Some repetitions will, therefore, be encountered, but only such portions are repeated as we felt needed repetition. It is my prayer that the readers may receive as great a blessing from reading these messages as I have personally received in preparing them. No series I have ever prepared has brought greater blessing and appreciation of the glories of Christ than this group on the tabernacle, and it is my hope that some of this inspiration has been carried along as they appear in printed form. May God bless them to His glory.

M. R. De Haan

Grand Rapids, Michigan

INTRODUCTION

THE tabernacle in the wilderness which became the center of all the worship of the children of Israel during their journeyings was designed by God Himself in heaven. Repeatedly Moses is admonished to follow the exact pattern (Exodus 25:40; Hebrews 8:5). It was, therefore, a perfect replica of something which already existed before in heaven. The tabernacle was a type and a shadow of something with real substance. Whether there is in heaven an actual building after which the tabernacle of God on earth was patterned is a debatable subject, but of one thing we are sure, the tabernacle is a picture, a type, and a shadow of the Lord Jesus Christ, where God meets man, and where deity and humanity meet in one person (Hebrews 8:1-2).

In Christ, therefore, we find the complete answer to the spiritual significance of this tabernacle. In John 1:14 it is said:

> And the Word was made flesh, and dwelt [tabernacled] among us, (and we beheld his glory, the glory as of the only begotten of the Father,) full of grace and truth.

Every detail of the tabernacle, therefore, points to some aspect of the person and work of our Saviour. It is the primary purpose of this volume to set forth the all-sufficient and perfect provision for redemption in Jesus Christ.

But in addition to being a picture of the Lord Jesus Christ, the tabernacle becomes secondarily, a picture of the believer. Jesus was the tabernacle in whom all the fullness of the Godhead dwelt bodily. The believer "IN CHRIST" is also the dwelling place of God. We are both "IN Christ" and

Christ is "IN US," the hope of glory. Our life is hid with Christ in God. We are, moreover, temples of the Holy Spirit. Just as the tabernacle was a dwelling place for God consisting of three compartments or rooms, so too the believer as the dwelling place of the Spirit is a trinity in unity. The redeemed person is composed of body, soul and spirit. The body corresponds to the court of the tabernacle. It is the outer, the visible part of our personality. It is the place of sacrifice (Romans 12:1-2). The soul answers to the holy place and is the place of worship and fellowship with other believers, feeding about the table, walking in the light, interceding for others. Finally, the spirit of the believer is the inner holy of holies, the deepest, hidden life of perfect, individual, personal communion with God beneath the blood. It is the place of spiritual victory.

But the tabernacle tells more. It is not only a picture of the Lord Jesus, and the believer, but it is a complete picture of the plan of salvation. It consists of seven steps. (1) As sinners on the outside we must enter through the door and stop first at the altar. The altar is the Cross, the starting point of our experience of salvation. (2) Next comes separation and daily cleansing at the laver. (3) We enter into the fellowship of the Word at the table. (4) We learn to walk in the light of the golden candlestick (I John 1:7). (5) Then and then only comes power in prayer at the incense altar. (6) We are then ready to enter the holy of holies to the highest service of the tabernacle, personal power and communion in our most innermost life. (7) Thus we reach perfect rest and peace at the blood-sprinkled mercy seat under the shadow of the cherubim.

The subject of the tabernacle is inexhaustible. In these messages we have merely touched the fringe of the limitless expanse of its infinite teachings. We have emphasized the

THE
TABERNACLE

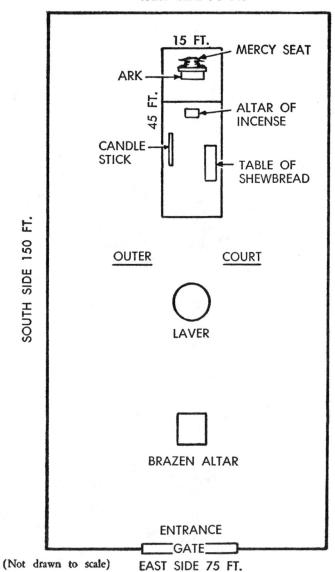

WEST SIDE 75 FT.

15 FT.

MERCY SEAT

ARK

45 FT.

ALTAR OF INCENSE

CANDLE STICK

TABLE OF SHEWBREAD

SOUTH SIDE 150 FT.

NORTH SIDE 150 FT.

OUTER   COURT

LAVER

BRAZEN ALTAR

ENTRANCE
GATE

(Not drawn to scale)   EAST SIDE 75 FT.

Chapter One

THE ARCHITECT OF SALVATION

And the Lord spake unto Moses, saying,

Speak unto the children of Israel, that they bring me an offering: of every man that giveth it willingly with his heart ye shall take my offering.

And let them make me a sanctuary; that I may dwell among them.

According to all that I shew thee, after the pattern of the tabernacle, and the pattern of all the instruments thereof, even so shall ye make it (Exodus 25:1, 2, 8, 9).

THE only building ever constructed upon this earth which was perfect from its very beginning and outset in every detail, and never again needed attention, addition or alteration, was the tabernacle in the wilderness. The blue print, the pattern and the plan, the design, and all of its specifications, were minutely made in heaven, committed unto Moses for the children of Israel, while he was in the mountain, shortly after their deliverance from Egypt. Every single detail was designed by Almighty God, every part had a prophetic, redemptive, and typical significance. There is no portion of Scripture richer in meaning, more perfect in its teaching of the plan of redemption, than this divinely designed building. God Himself was the architect, and every detail points to some aspect of the character and work of the person of His Son, Jesus Christ, and, in its complete form, it is probably the most comprehensive, detailed revelation of Jesus the Son of God, and the plan of salvation in the entire Old Testament.

SMALL STRUCTURE

It was not an imposing structure from the exterior, and its unattractive outside gave little hint of its inner glory and beauty. A stranger viewing it from without would see none of the exquisite beauty and the breath-taking splendor of its glorious interior. Only after one had entered through the door at its eastern end, stopped to sacrifice at the altar of burnt offering, had washed his hands and feet at the laver, could one enter to behold the interior of this most magnificent "house of God."

Before taking you into some of the glories of this interior, we would first of all have you get a clear mental picture of the structure as a whole. Imagine, therefore, first of all, a rectangular plot of ground, 75 feet wide and 150 feet long. This is the size of an ordinary city lot. This rectangular lot was enclosed by a fence, seven and one-half feet high, surrounding the three sides, the north, the south, and the west. At the eastern end of this enclosure was the gate of the court, the only means of entrance into this sacred area. This gate was thirty feet wide, all the rest being enclosed by this white linen fence, suspended like a curtain on brazen pillars, the pillars themselves resting upon a foundation of brazen sockets. This enclosure was later called the

COURT OF THE GENTILES

This court of the Gentiles always faced to the east, toward the rising of the sun, for it was a clear type of, and pointed forward to, the Sun of Righteousness, the Lord Jesus Christ our Saviour. At the eastern end of this court, just inside the gate or door, stood a brazen altar and to the west of this stood the brazen laver or wash basin, containing water for the cleansing of the worshipers before they entered into the holy place of the tabernacle. These, the altar and the laver, were the only two items of furniture in this open, roofless court, surrounding the tabernacle proper.

The tabernacle itself was a flat-roofed, rectangular, tent-

like building, located at the western end of this enclosure
which we have described, and already referred to as the
outer court. It was a portable building, fifteen feet wide,
fifteen feet high, and forty-five feet long, about the size of
an extra-large living room. This space was divided into two
unequal compartments. The front room, facing the east,
was thirty feet long and fifteen feet wide and fifteen feet
high. This was called the holy place, or the first sanctuary.
The rear room (separated by a veil from the holy place)
was in the shape of a perfect cube, fifteen by fifteen by
fifteen feet. This was called the holy of holies, or the most
holy place.

The Furnishings

In the holy place, the larger of the two rooms, were three
pieces of furniture; the dining table on the north side, the
lamp on the south side, and between these and slightly to
the rear, was the altar of incense. In the smaller room,
called the holy of holies, and behind the veil which hid
them from view, stood the ark of the covenant and the
mercy seat. There were thus exactly seven pieces of furniture, speaking of the perfection of Him, to which all these
pointed. Every part of this building, every article of furniture, pointed to some aspect of the perfection of the personality and ministry of the Lord Jesus Christ, our meeting place with God, our "tabernacle."

These articles of furniture were so arranged that if we
draw a straight line from the altar at the door at the eastern
end, to the ark in the holiest place, bisecting the incense
altar, and then draw a line at right angles to this line from
the dining table on the north side to the lamp on the south
side, we have a perfect figure of the Cross; for all of this
speaks of one thing, the beginning of our salvation, and
the work of Christ performed for us upon the Cross of
Calvary.

The furniture of the tabernacle proper was all of the finest

gold, its hangings, curtains and coverings of the most exquisite needle work in white linen and purple and blue
and scarlet.

THE WALLS

The walls of this building were made of gold-plated upright boards, which stood vertically, each upon two sockets
of silver. The boards, made of acacia wood, were completely
covered with gold, each board fifteen feet long and two and
one-fourth feet wide. There were twenty boards each for the
two long sides of the tabernacle, and six boards for the
western wall. These boards stood upright, next to one another, in their silver sockets (which were imbedded in the
desert sand), and were united by five horizontal gold-plated
bars which passed through golden loops attached to the
boards, from end to end, thus uniting them all into one
solid, rigid wall. The inside of the tabernacle, therefore,
was decorated with solid gold on all of its four sides.

THE ROOF

The roof of this tabernacle was made of four layers of
cloth and leather. First, on the inside and forming the
ceiling of the tabernacle, and the only one of the four
coverings visible from within, was the linen covering, beautifully embroidered with gold, purple, blue and scarlet, and
with figures of cherubim looking down upon the worshiper.
This linen sheet covered the tabernacle. Over this linen
covering which formed the ceiling of the tabernacle proper,
was next placed a covering of cloth made of goats' hair,
which slightly overlapped the linen curtains. Over this was
draped a covering of rams' skins dyed a bright red, and
over this and forming the outer covering was a great curtain of leather made of badger skins, drab, gray and un-
impressive, but water and weather repellent.

In succeeding chapters we shall go into detail concerning
the meaning and the typical teachings of all of these various

parts, their construction, and their arrangement. In this opening and introductory message we want you first of all to get the overall picture, a clear image of the general structure of this curious building and its arrangement. The stranger, standing on the outside of this building, could see only two things, the white linen fence surrounding the court, and the top part or roof of the tabernacle itself. Since the top or roof was covered with a leather curtain of drab gray badger skins, the outsider would see none of the inner beauty. There was no hint to the viewer on the outside, of the breathless, exquisite beauty which met the eyes of those who had gained entrance through the door, by way of the altar.

The person on the outside, of course, represents the sinner, the natural man without Christ, in the wilderness of sin. The priest on the inside represents the believer who has passed through the door, and appropriated the blood of the sacrifice at the altar and been washed by the water of the Word in the brazen laver. He can truly be said to be "in Christ," for the tabernacle is a picture of the Lord Jesus Christ.

Both the sinner on the outside, and the saint on the inside see Christ, but how differently they behold Him! The sinner (the man on the outside) sees the linen fence, to be sure, but that bars his entrance to the tabernacle, and keeps him outside. He sees the badger skins, drab gray, unattractive and dull. The white linen speaks of Christ's perfect righteousness. White linen speaks of righteousness in Scripture wherever it is used. This the unregenerate man can easily see. Even the infidel and the unbeliever admit, and must admit the perfections of Christ morally. The unregenerate student of the Bible sees and admits that Christ was not an ordinary man. He admires His ideal moral character, extols His wisdom and teachings, but does not see His deity, His virgin birth, His atonement, His precious blood, resurrection, or coming again. This only the believer who has entered the gate can see. Until a man, therefore, is born again, he cannot *see*, he cannot see more in Christ than His perfect humanity, His moral perfection, and His suffering.

Besides the linen curtain, the outsider also sees the dark badger skin roof of the tabernacle proper. This is Christ in His humanity, in which He was clothed while He was here on the earth. It is His humanity exposed to the desert storms of hate, reviling and abuse of mankind. Isaiah says of the humanity of Christ:

> He hath no form nor comeliness; and when we shall see him, there is no beauty that we should desire him (Isaiah 53:2).

Here, indeed, is a picture of the sinner and his view of the Lord Jesus Christ. The Bible says that

> the natural man receiveth not the things of the Spirit of God: for they are foolishness unto him: neither can he know them, because they are spiritually discerned (I Corinthians 2:14).

And again:

> In whom the god of this world hath blinded the minds of them which believe not, lest the light of the glorious gospel of Christ, who is the image of God, should shine unto them (II Corinthians 4:4).

But there was one way to enter this tabernacle, and behold its inner glory, and only one way. It was through the one and only gate which stood before the altar of sacrifice. The white linen of God's perfect righteousness prohibits the sinner from ever approaching God in his own goodness and morality and righteousness, but there was, nevertheless a way, through the door, which is the Lord Jesus Christ. Our Saviour Himself said:

> I am the door: by me if any man enter in, he shall be saved (John 10:9).

Again, He said:

> I am the way, the truth, and the life: no man cometh unto the Father, but by me (John 14:6).

And when the sinner enters that door, he comes face to face, first with the altar of burnt offering, a perfect picture of the Cross where the Lord Jesus Christ made atonement for sin, and next, the laver of cleansing, to wash away all that sin, and then, and then only can one enter through the veil into His presence to feed at His table, walk in the light of the golden candlestick, and learn to minister to others at the golden incense altar.

The tabernacle, therefore, was both inclusive and exclusive. It excluded all those who refused to come by the one and only door. The linen fence barred access to the sinner as long as he had one single sin upon him; as long as there was a single spot of imperfection in his being, he was prohibited from approaching the tabernacle; he was barred by the perfect demand of God's holy righteousness and God's holy law. Access could only be gained by coming by faith through the door and appropriating the blood of the substitute slain upon the altar, and then he could truly be said to be "in Christ." As the tabernacle excluded the sinner, so it was inclusive for the believer and made him absolutely safe, because he was shut in with God Himself. As Noah himself was shut in by God, and God Himself closed the door, so those who by faith come to the Lord Jesus Christ are shut in, and of them He says:

> And I give unto them eternal life; and they shall never perish, neither shall any man pluck them out of my hand (John 10:28).

Have you ever come by that door? You may be religious, admire Christ as a perfect man, worship His goodness, virtues and graces, but until you come alone as a poor sinner, and appropriate the blood of faith, there is no hope and no salvation.

Chapter Two

LAW AND GRACE IN SALVATION

> And he said unto Moses, Come up unto the Lord, thou, and Aaron, Nadab, and Abihu, and seventy of the elders of Israel; and worship ye afar off.
>
> And Moses alone shall come near the Lord: but they shall not come nigh; neither shall the people go up with him.
>
> And Moses went into the midst of the cloud, and gat him up into the mount: and Moses was in the mount forty days and forty nights (Exodus 24:1, 2, 18).

BEFORE an individual can be saved, he must first learn that he cannot save himself. Adam had to learn this tremendous lesson. After he had sinned, he imagined that he could get rid of his sin with a self-made garment of fig-leaf aprons. But God came down and ignored his flimsy fig leaves, and pronounced the curse upon him, and upon all his offspring and creation. And then, and then only it is that God showed him the only way, by providing God's own remedy, when He (God) slew an animal and took the skins of the bloody victim, and clothed Adam and his wife (Genesis 3:21) with the substitutionary skins. This is ever God's order. It has never changed. He kills before He makes alive. He first brings down, before He brings up. He makes poor before He makes rich (I Samuel 2:6-7).

SAME IN TABERNACLE

This same order is followed in the giving of the tabernacle to Israel in the wilderness. The record of the pattern of this tabernacle is found in Exodus 25 to 31. Its actual construction is recorded in Exodus 35 to 40. The instruction for the building, however, is preceded by the record of the giving of the law of God. The record of the actual building of the tabernacle is also preceded by a repetition of the story of the giving of the law, and the sad, sad record of Israel's miserable failure in the worship of the golden calf. Before Moses brought the two tables of the law down from the Mount, Israel had already broken them, and were under the sentence of death, and the judgment of God. Notice, therefore, carefully the order of the story in Exodus 19 to 40. In Exodus 19 to 24 we have a detailed account of the commandments, statutes, precepts and laws which God enjoined through Moses upon Israel. These laws were designed to show Israel their utter inability to keep God's commandments, or to be saved by their own righteousness. But poor blinded Israel, in their depraved condition, deceived by sin in their self-righteousness, supposed that they could keep them perfectly, and so we read:

> And Moses came and told the people all the words of the Lord, and all the judgments: and all the people answered with one voice, and said, All the words which the Lord hath said will we do (Exodus 24:3).

Poor, poor blinded souls! They stood before God's holy law and said, "We can keep that law — ALL THE WORDS WHICH THE LORD HATH SAID WE WILL DO." How little they knew and understood and realized their own hearts and their own inability. But Moses recognized how blind they were, and so immediately after this foolish promise of Israel to be saved by their own works, and by perfect obedience to God's perfect commandments, he is quick to offer an atonement. Notice, therefore, carefully in the next verse:

> And Moses wrote all the words of the Lord, and rose up early in the morning, and builded an altar under the hill (Exodus 24:4).

Realizing that Israel could be saved, *not* by keeping the law, but only by the blood of a sacrifice, he builds an altar immediately, and then the record continues:

> And he sent young men of the children of Israel, which offered burnt offerings, and sacrificed peace offerings of oxen unto the Lord.
>
> And Moses took half of the blood, and put it in basons; and half of the blood he sprinkled on the altar.
>
> And he took the book of the covenant, and read in the audience of the people: and they said, ALL THAT THE LORD HATH SAID WILL WE DO, AND BE OBEDIENT (Exodus 24:5-7).

Still they did not understand the meaning of this sprinkling of the blood and the death of the sacrifices. When Moses read the law the first time they foolishly said, "Yes, we can keep that law. We don't need a Saviour. We can save ourselves by our own good works, and obedience, by keeping God's law." And then Moses offers the sacrifices and sprinkles the blood to show the need for mercy and not for justice, and that they could not save themselves, apart from the blood. If they had been able to keep God's law perfectly, they would have needed no sacrifice, no substitute, no blood. But they missed the lesson entirely, and so Moses reads the law again to them, with the same result, for again they say:

> All that the Lord hath said WILL WE DO, AND BE OBEDIENT (Exodus 24:7).

Now notice the response of the Lord through Moses. Instead of the Lord saying, "All right, you can keep that law, and so you can save yourself, and therefore, need no Redeemer, no atonement," we read instead,

> And Moses took the blood, and sprinkled it on the people, and said, BEHOLD THE BLOOD OF THE COVENANT, which the Lord hath made with you concerning all these words (Exodus 24:8).

BEHOLD THE BLOOD

God's answer to Israel's foolish promise, "All that the Lord hath said will we do" is "BEHOLD THE BLOOD." What Israel needed was grace, mercy, *not* their own righteousness and achievement. And then it is that Moses goes again up into the mountain and was in the mountain forty days and forty nights. We have given you all this introductory information to show you the setting for the giving of the tabernacle. And when Moses came down from the mountain, what do you suppose he brought back with him? The law? Ah, no, but something far better than the law; it was the pattern of the tabernacle; the picture of grace; the plan of salvation in the Lord Jesus Christ and glorious type of our substitute and redeemer; the tabernacle with its blood from top to bottom, and end to end, from the altar to the mercy seat.

I trust, therefore, that you get the picture which God seeks to paint for us in this passage. When Moses went up into Mt. Sinai, he received more than the tables of the law, and the commandments, statutes and precepts. Were this all that Moses brought back, the story of Israel would have ended right there. For before Moses descended with the law, Israel had already broken its every commandment in the worship of the golden calf. And the law, perfect, holy, just, demanded death and judgment of the transgressors. Had Moses, therefore, brought only the law, we repeat, the story would have ended right here in the total destruction of the nation of Israel. But in addition to the law, Moses brought back the blueprint for the tabernacle, God's provision for a sinful people, God's answer to a broken law, God's wonderful plan of salvation for hell-deserving sinners.

And so Exodus 25 begins by telling us what Moses received in the mountain. Remember, therefore, that God gave to Israel through Moses in the mountain, two things:

I. The law.

II. The tabernacle.

The law — to show the awfulness of sin, and man's desperate failure; the tabernacle — to show God's way out for the guilty ones who had broken His holy law. God gave first the law which speaks of God's justice, holiness, condemnation, and penalty of death. "For by the law is the knowledge of sin." Had God given no more to Israel, she would have perished immediately. But the Lord foreknew Israel's failure, He foresaw their need of the blood, He knew they could not keep the holy law, and so He gave in addition, the tabernacle which speaks of mercy, pardon, forgiveness, atonement, redemption, and salvation, for all who would admit that they could not save themselves by their own efforts and works, and by the keeping of the law.

SAME ORDER REPEATED

Now this same identical order is repeated again in Exodus 32 to 40. After Moses had given the pattern of the tabernacle to Israel in Exodus 25 to 31, the actual construction is described in Exodus 35 to 40. But sandwiched between the giving of the pattern of the tabernacle in chapters 25 to 31, and the actual record of its building and construction in chapters 35 to 40, we have three chapters recording the broken law, and the giving of the second tables of the law, and then follows the actual rearing of the building.

We have gone into all of this detail, which may at first seem uninteresting, but it is important, in order to show the setting in which the tabernacle was given to Israel. It was God's revelation of His plan of salvation by grace, and redemption through faith. But first, He must show them how far short they came, allow them to prove the utter depravity of the human heart, convince them of their total corruption, and then, and then only, are they ready for the message of grace. Paul voices this very thing in Titus 3:5,

> Not by works of righteousness which we have done, but according to his mercy he saved us, by the washing of regeneration, and renewing of the Holy Ghost.

And so, before we take up in detail the study of the tabernacle proper, we want you to remember the setting, and the fact that God gave to Israel two things in the mountain: the law—to condemn, to convict of sin, and to convince man of his own helplessness; and secondly, the pattern of the tabernacle—to show God's remedy for sin, that they might turn from the law to grace, from Sinai to Calvary, from their own righteousness to God's righteousness, from their own DOING to God's DONE.

> For what the law could not do, in that it was weak through the flesh, God sending his own Son in the likeness of sinful flesh, and for sin, condemned sin in the flesh (Romans 8:3).

After some thirty-five hundred years of human history, man still has not learned this tremendous lesson, but is still seeking by his own goodness and effort in the keeping of the law to be saved and made righteous in the sight of God. He insists upon resting upon his own morality, his religion, his law works, to please God, and says in essence with Israel,

> All that the Lord hath said WILL WE DO.

I want to emphasize in closing this message, three words which Israel in her blindness repeated over and over again. WE WILL DO! WE WILL DO! That is man's vain dream, and has been ever since man first fell. But God comes and says, "What you do, will not do." Man's best comes far short of God's lowest and least requirements. And so He sent His Son, the Lord Jesus Christ, into the world in fulfillment of the type of the tabernacle, and He bore our sins, and shed His blood, and now the message of grace is, IT IS DONE! IT IS DONE! And this finished work of the Lord Jesus Christ, fully developed in the New Testament, was already given in shadow and in type and revealed in the picture of the tabernacle, with its altar, with its blood, with its sacrifices, its provision for every need of the human heart.

And so in closing, we want to quote the Holy Spirit's own testimony in the New Testament concerning the tabernacle in the wilderness:

> For when Moses had spoken every precept to all the people according to the law, he took the blood of calves and of goats,

> with water, and scarlet wool, and hyssop, and sprinkled both the book, and all the people,
>
> Saying, This is the blood of the testament which God hath enjoined unto you.
>
> Moreover he sprinkled with blood both the tabernacle, and all the vessels of the ministry.
>
> And almost all things are by the law purged with blood; and without shedding of blood is no remission (Hebrews 9: 19-22).

The personal question is, Have you learned the lesson of trusting only in the finished work of the Lord Jesus Christ? There is no salvation until you quit working for your salvation. There is nothing that can be done. The sinner is hopeless and helpless to be saved by his own efforts, his own religion, his own merits, his own goodness, his own morality, his own righteousness. He must come as a poor, bankrupt pauper, and hell-deserving sinner, to the foot of the Cross for the grace and mercy of the Lord Jesus Christ.

The Apostle Paul nails it down so that there can be no question about it, when in Romans 4:5 he says:

> But to him that worketh not, but believeth on him that justifieth the ungodly, his faith is counted for righteousness.

Have you learned the lesson? Are you resting in His work, or are you still trusting in your own work? Have you ever come as a poor, lost sinner, claiming absolutely nothing, but the grace of God and the blood of the Lord Jesus Christ? If not, will you do it now?

Chapter Three

WHERE GOD MEETS MAN

THE tabernacle God commanded Moses to build in the wilderness, shortly after Israel's deliverance from Egypt was a perfect type and a figure of the Lord Jesus Christ. He is the more perfect, eternal dwelling place of God, and it was after this pattern of the Lord Jesus that every part and detail of this tabernacle was designed. We believe, therefore, that every detail of this structure, the materials, the furniture, and the ministry in the tabernacle, revealed some particular aspect of the infinite graces, virtues, attributes, personality, and work of our Saviour. This is made clear in Hebrews. In Hebrews 9 the writer gives a brief description of this tabernacle, and says:

> For there was a tabernacle made; the first, wherein was the candlestick, and the table, and the shewbread; which is called the sanctuary (Hebrews 9:2).

This was the larger of the two rooms in the tabernacle, called the sanctuary, or the holy place. Sanctuary means "holy place."

Then follows the writer's description of the other smaller room, called the holy of holies, or the most holy place. In Hebrews 9 he continues:

> And after the second veil, [which separated the holy place from the holy of holies], the tabernacle which is called the Holiest of all;
>
> Which had the golden censer, and the ark of the covenant overlaid round about with gold, wherein was the golden pot that had manna, and Aaron's rod that budded, and the tables of the covenant;

And over it the cherubims of glory shadowing the mercy seat; of which we cannot now speak particularly (Hebrews 9:3-5).

But Christ being come an high priest of good things to come, by a greater and more perfect tabernacle, not made with hands, that is to say, not of this building;

Neither by the blood of goats and calves, but by his own blood he entered in once into the holy place, having obtained eternal redemption for us.

For if the blood of bulls and of goats, and the ashes of an heifer sprinkling the unclean, sanctifieth to the purifying of the flesh:

How much more shall the blood of Christ, who through the eternal Spirit offered himself without spot to God, purge your conscience from dead works to serve the living God? (Hebrews 9:11-14).

Before taking up the typical teaching of this figure of Christ in the Old Testament, we want to stop for a moment to study the meaning of the word "tabernacle" itself. It is called the "tabernacle of witness" in Numbers 17. In Revelation 15:5 it is called the "tabernacle of testimony." It was the one and only place where God witnessed and testified to Israel their duty and responsibility to Him. In Exodus 33:7 we have the expression, "tabernacle of the congregation." This was not the tabernacle we are discussing, but a temporary tent used by Israel while awaiting the construction of the real tabernacle. But the phrase, "tabernacle of the congregation," expresses perfectly the nature of this building. A congregation is a meeting of individuals for fellowship and counsel, and thus, the tabernacle is called "the tent of meeting." It was the place where man met God, and God met man. It is the meeting place of God and man, and note well, it was the *only* place where man could approach God, and where God would meet with man, upon the basis and the sacrifice and the blood. There was no other place of meeting designated in Israel, except the place of sacrifice and shedding of blood in the tabernacle.

What a picture of our precious Lord. He is the perfect

tabernacle, and IN HIM man can approach God, and IN
HIM, and Him alone God condescends to meet with man
on the basis of the blood of the sacrifice. And it is the only
place, the only way of approach to God, for only in Christ
can God and the sinner meet, on the ground of His shed
blood. There is no question about the Scripturalness of
this interpretation, for turning again to Hebrews 9:6-7 we
read:

> Now when these things were thus ordained [the building
> of the tabernacle], the priests went always into the first taber-
> nacle, accomplishing the service of God.
> But into the second [the Holy of Holies] went the high
> priest alone once every year, not without blood, which he
> offered for himself, and for the errors of the people.

Now notice carefully what this represented. The author
of Hebrews continues and gives us the Holy Spirit's own
interpretation of all of these things.

> The Holy Ghost this signifying, that the way into the
> holiest of all was not yet made manifest, while as the first
> tabernacle was yet standing:
> Which was a figure [type] for the time then present (He-
> brews 9:8-9).

TABERNACLE A TYPE

Here then is the Holy Spirit's own testimony and witness,
that the tabernacle in the wilderness was a figure of something future, yet to come. The word "figure" means "type,"
or "shadow," and so we are reminded that this tabernacle
was only a shadow of something greater which still lay in
the future. And here it is:

> But Christ being come an high priest of good things TO
> COME, by a greater and more perfect tabernacle [his body],
> not made with hands, that is to say, not of this building;
> Neither by the blood of goats and calves, but by his own
> blood he entered in once into the holy place, having obtained
> eternal redemption for us.
> For if the blood of bulls and of goats, and the ashes of an
> heifer sprinkling the unclean, sanctifieth to the purifying of
> the flesh:

> How much more shall the blood of Christ, who through the eternal Spirit offered himself without spot to God, purge your conscience from dead works to serve the living God? (Hebrews 9:11-14).

Christ, therefore, is the original tabernacle, eternal in the heavens. The tabernacle in the wilderness was a figure and a shadow of Him who was still to come. The altar speaks of Him on the Cross. The laver speaks of Him as the eternal Word; the table of shewbread as Christ the Bread of life; the lamp as Christ the Light of the world; the incense altar speaks of our interceding High Priest. The ark speaks of His supreme authority and kingly position and finished work; the wood in the tabernacle points to His humanity; the gold to His deity; the silver to His blood; the brass to His perfect holiness. Purple speaks of His royalty; white of His righteousness; scarlet of His sacrifice, and of His blood. The veil points to His body which must be rent to give access to God. And so we might go on and on, for we believe that every single part in every detail in this tabernacle in some way pre-figured and foreshadowed some aspect of the infinite work of the Lord Jesus Christ.

ONLY ONE PLACE

But let me remind you again that there was only *one* tabernacle, only *one* tent of meeting, only *one* place of sacrifice. The Lord would not accept any sacrifice, no matter how perfect, which was not brought upon the altar in this *one and only* tabernacle. In Leviticus 17:3 and 4 we read:

> What man soever there be of the house of Israel, that killeth an ox, or lamb, or goat . . .
> And bringeth it not unto the door of the tabernacle of the congregation, to offer an offering unto the Lord before the tabernacle of the Lord . . . that man shall be cut off from among his people.

There was only one place of sacrifice permitted, and that was at the altar in the gate of the tabernacle. It was the sin of Israel in repeatedly sacrificing in other places, in

groves and upon high hills, which provoked the displeasure
of the Lord and brought judgment upon them, and caused
them finally to be dispersed among the nations. There is
today still only one way to God, only one place where God
will meet with the sinner. This is prefigured by the tabernacle in the wilderness, and it is the Lord Jesus Christ, and
at the Cross of Calvary. He said:

> I am the way, the truth, and the life: no man cometh unto
> the Father, but by me (John 14:6).

The Apostle Peter after Pentecost declares:

> Neither is there salvation in any other: for there is none
> other name under heaven given among men, whereby we
> must be saved (Acts 4:12).

Failure on the part of Israel to come only by way of the
altar in the tabernacle resulted in the curse of God upon
them. And this is just as true today, for the Bible has not
changed, and God has not changed. Seeking to find favor
with God through our own efforts, our own merit, our own
goodness, religion, and our works, leaves man only under
the curse of God, and the sentence of eternal death. Religion, morality, ethics, good works, ordinances and charity,
sincere as they may be, cannot substitute for faith in Christ,
and the blood shed on the Cross. Without faith in Him,
without His blood, these are merely dead works.

ONE MORE LESSON

Before concluding this chapter we would point to one
other great teaching in the type of the tabernacle. It is not
alone the only place where God and the sinner can meet
in Christ, but in the tabernacle, deity and humanity met
in one perfect whole. The boards, the altar, the pillars of
the tabernacle, were made of two materials, wood and
gold. The wood was the incorruptible desert wood, acacia
or shittim wood, and the gold was pure, refined gold. The
wood of this tree was the only kind of wood which was
permitted in the construction of the building.

> And thou shalt make boards for the tabernacle of shittim wood standing up (Exodus 26:15).

These boards were made from a tree which grew sparsely in the desert regions through which they passed. It was the result of growth under most adverse circumstances. It represented the "humanity of Christ." It is the man, Christ Jesus, born of a virgin, as a root out of dry ground, growing up as a tender plant (Isaiah 53:2). It was an unattractive tree, as prefiguring Him of whom it was said, "He hath no form nor comeliness, and when we shall see him, there is no beauty that we should desire him" (Isaiah 53:2). It points definitely to Him of whom John said:

> And the Word was made flesh, and dwelt [tabernacled] among us (John 1:14).

But these boards were overlaid with pure gold.

> And thou shalt overlay the boards with gold (Exodus 26:29).

Gold in Scripture symbolically points to deity. It was the most precious metal then known to man. Each board, therefore, in the tabernacle was wood, overlaid with pure gold, yet one single board. What a figure of the mystery of "God manifest in the flesh"; Jesus Christ, the Lord of glory, perfect God, and yet perfect man; two natures, and yet only one person; not two persons, but one; not half God and half man, but perfect man and perfect God in one single person, the Saviour, the Lord Jesus Christ. Of Him John says later:

> In the beginning was the Word, and the Word was with God, and the Word was God.
>
> The same was in the beginning with God.
>
> All things were made by him; and without him was not any thing made that was made.
>
> And the Word was made flesh, and dwelt among us, (and we beheld his glory, the glory as of the only begotten of the Father,) full of grace and truth (John 1:1-3, 14).

A MYSTERY

This indeed is a deep mystery, and we cannot understand it, for it must be ever accepted by faith alone. Paul tells us it is a mystery in Colossians 1:19,

> For it pleased the Father that in him should all fulness dwell.

Again Paul says of him in I Timothy 3:16,

> And without controversy great is the mystery of godliness: God was manifest in the flesh, justified in the Spirit, seen of angels, preached unto the Gentiles, believed on in the world, received up into glory.

This then is the picture of the Lord Jesus Christ, as represented in the two basic materials in the structure of the tabernacle. It is the only kind of a person who could be a redeemer, for He is the God-Man, who alone can bring God and man together in perfect harmony. He is the tent of meeting, where perfect humanity and perfect deity meet in one person, so that as man, He could pay for man's sin; as God He could pay the infinite price — not for one, but for all. He is like a ladder, resting upon the earth among men by His humanity, reaching up into heaven by His deity; like a bridge spanning the river of destruction, one end resting on the brink of doom and the other settled on the shore of heaven.

The redeemer *must* be both God and man to be a mediator who can bridge the gulf by dying like a man, and rising from the dead as the eternal God. The writer of Hebrews sums it up in Hebrews 9:15 when he says:

> And for this cause he is the mediator of the new testament, that by means of death, for the redemption of the transgressions that were under the first testament, they which are called might receive the promise of eternal inheritance.

There is, then, no other place where man can meet God, where God can be reconciled, and man can be saved, than in the person of the Lord Jesus Christ. Again we repeat,

> Neither is there salvation in any other: for there is none other name under heaven given among men, whereby we must be saved (Acts 4:12).

Chapter Four

WHOSOEVER WILL MAY COME

THE most costly building, for its size, ever erected, was the tabernacle in the wilderness. Though only forty-five feet long, and fifteen feet wide, and having only two rooms, one the size of an ordinary living room, and the other the size of a bedroom, its cost is estimated to have exceeded two million dollars. All of its framework and its furniture was overlaid with pure gold. All of this points, of course, to the preciousness and infinite value and worth of the Lord Jesus Christ our Saviour, of whom the tabernacle was a figure and a shadow, according to the New Testament. From this tabernacle every one was excluded except those who came by the way of the door and the blood and the altar at the entrance of the tabernacle. It stood within an enclosure the size of a city lot, and was bounded by a white linen fence seven and one-half feet high, suspended on sixty pillars or posts of solid brass, resting upon sockets of brass. This enclosure was called the court of the tabernacle.

> And thou shalt make the court of the tabernacle: for the south side southward there shall be hangings for the court of fine twined linen of an hundred cubits long for one side:
>
> And the twenty pillars thereof and their twenty sockets . . .
>
> And likewise for the north side . . .
>
> And for the breadth of the court on the west side shall be hangings of fifty cubits . . .
>
> And for the breadth of the court on the east side eastward shall be fifty cubits (Exodus 27:9-13).

PURPOSE OF FENCE

Now the purpose of this fence was to keep man out. Man's approach to the tabernacle where God dwelt was barred completely by the linen fence which surrounded it. White linen, of course, speaks of God's perfect righteousness. The brass pillars point to God's judgment upon sin. God's perfect holiness prevents and forbids man from coming unto God, as long as he has sin upon him. This fence, therefore, was of pure white linen. God's demands are perfect obedience. God gave expression to this perfect righteousness in the tables of the law which He gave by the hand of Moses. The law demands perfect obedience. One single sin is enough to condemn man before God, for James says:

> For whosoever shall keep the whole law, and yet offend in one point, he is guilty of all (James 2:10).

By comparison with God's perfect righteousness, all of man's good works, righteousness, morality, are like filthy rags. The law is not the way to God, but instead it bars the sinner from coming to God until the sin question has been taken care of. It says, "Do this, or die. Keep this, or perish." The law was never designed to save a single individual, or to keep anyone saved, but rather to cause us to look elsewhere, outside of self and away from the demands of the law for our salvation. Paul tells us clearly:

> For what the law could not do, in that it was weak through the flesh (Romans 8:3).

The linen fence then separated the camp of Israel from the presence of the Lord God. It represented the law. It said, Stay out, keep away, no admittance.

THE DOOR

But there was a way provided for the sinner whereby he could approach from the outside and enter into communion and fellowship with God. He could not come over the fence, or under or through it, but by means of a door especially provided. At the eastern end of this enclosure was a wide gate which gave entrance to the tabernacle where God dwelt.

And the hanging [curtain] for the gate [door] of the court was needlework, of blue, and purple, and scarlet, and fine twined linen: and twenty cubits was the length, and the height in the breadth was five cubits (Exodus 38:18).

This was the only opening in the linen fence, and the only way of approach to the tabernacle. It was an opening thirty feet long, seven and one-half feet high, made of white linen, beautifully embroidered with blue and scarlet and purple needlework. The door, of course, points to the Lord Jesus Christ as the only approach to God; for He Himself said centuries later:

I am the door: by me if any man enter in, he shall be saved (John 10:9).

In John 14:6 He says:

I am the way, the truth, and the life: no man cometh unto the Father, but by me.

To this also Peter refers, when in Acts 4:12 he says to the members of the Sanhedrin:

Neither is there salvation in any other: for there is none other name under heaven given among men, whereby we must be saved.

Four Colors

The curtain which hung across this gate likewise speaks of Him who is the Door into the sheepfold, for this curtain was made of fine white linen, and worked into its texture in fine needlework were patterns of purple and scarlet and blue. These were the four prominent colors of the tabernacle, and each one points to some particular aspect of the nature and character of the person of our Saviour. Purple is the sign of royalty, the color of the King. Scarlet is the color of blood, and speaks of sacrifice. White is, as we have noted, the color of perfection, and righteousness; while blue is the color of heaven.

As applied to the Lord Jesus Christ these four colors speak

of Christ in a fourfold way as the King, as a sacrificing Servant, as a perfect Man, and as perfect God. They suggest the picture of Christ in the four records of the Gospel by Matthew, Mark, Luke and John. Matthew corresponds to the purple, and tells us of Christ as the King of Israel. Mark corresponds to the scarlet, and presents Christ as the suffering Servant. Luke presents to us the perfect, sinless humanity of Christ Jesus and corresponds to the white linen, while John introduces us to the heaven-sent Son of God, the eternal Creator, aptly suggested by the blue color in the hangings of the court.

ONLY ONE DOOR

These four records constitute the Gospel of the grace of God. There is, after all, only one Gospel, the good news concerning the death and the resurrection of Jesus Christ for poor lost sinners. There are various aspects of this one Gospel, and we, therefore, read of the Gospel of the kingdom, and the Gospel of the grace of God, the everlasting Gospel and "my Gospel," but after all, each one of them refers to the same good news of Christ crucified, buried, and risen again for our redemption. This one Gospel is presented to us by four separate human authors. Matthew was a Jew and wrote particularly to Israel concerning the King of Israel. This is the purple Gospel. Mark was a Roman, and wrote especially for the Romans concerning the suffering servant. This was the scarlet Gospel. Luke was a Greek and wrote to the Greek mind, in the most beautiful, perfect Greek — the white Gospel, while John, the representative of the Christian Church, wrote of the heavenly character and origin of the Lord Jesus Christ, the Son of God — the blue Gospel story.

WHY FOUR GOSPELS

We ask, therefore, the question, "Why four Gospel records instead of only one?" And we believe that we find the answer in the gate of the tabernacle of the congregation in the wilderness. It was a wide gate — thirty feet wide. Its hangings were in four colors. It is the "whosoever" gate, through the person of the Lord Jesus Christ, and faith in Him. None are excluded and all may enter. In the days when the New Testament was written there were four kinds of people in Palestine. First of all, there were the Jews who had given the world its religious pattern, and the Word of God. Secondly, there were the Romans who had conquered Israel, and were the symbol of conquest and of power; and thirdly, there were the Greeks who gave the world its culture and its language, and the highest in art, architecture and literature, and then finally, that small group of believers whom we know today as Christians.

To these four groups, Jews, Romans, Greeks and believers, the four Gospels of the gate of the tabernacle are addressed. Matthew is addressed to the Jews; Mark to the Romans; Luke to the Greeks; and John is particularly to the Church. So you see that none are overlooked or excluded, but all of them have provision made whereby they may enter. The gate to the tabernacle into the presence of God is wide enough for all, is universal in its invitation, is all-inclusive in its appeal. All of it points to Him, who later on said:

> Come unto me, ALL ye that labour and are heavy laden, and I will give you rest (Matthew 11:28).

This then is the message of the fence and the gate of the tabernacle. The fence of the law says "stay out," but the door of the grace of God in Christ says, "Come in, whosoever will."

In conclusion, therefore, we emphasize again that there was only ONE DOOR, and it is the door of the person of the Lord Jesus Christ, the King, the Servant, the Man, the God of the universe. There is no other way to God than by personal faith in the Lord Jesus Christ, the Son of God. For He Himself says in John 10:1,

> Verily, verily, I say unto you, He that entereth not by the door into the sheepfold, but climbeth up some other way, the same is a thief and a robber (John 10:1).

Satan has invented myriads of other ways by which he claims that man can approach God, but all of them are the ways of deception, and lead only to eternal destruction. The Bible says, "There is a way that seemeth right to a man, but the end thereof are the ways of death." The Lord Jesus Christ describes it as the "broad way" upon which many travel on their way to destruction and doom.

Today we are living in an age of great and unprecedented deception, and there are thousands of strange voices being raised, calling out to the sinner, "This is the way, this is the way"; and yet, we remind you that the Lord Jesus Christ excludes all of them when He says, "I am the way; by me if any man enter in, he shall be saved." "There is none other name given" whereby we can obtain salvation, than by personal faith in the Lord Jesus Christ. It is, therefore, necessary and imperative that we shall be clear and definite in our teaching of the Word of God, lest those who are careless be deceived by the many strange voices active in the world today, and be led astray, and find out at the end of the road that it was all only deception, and a delusion.

And so we want to emphasize again the simplicity of the Gospel of salvation. The ABC's of salvation which we have given before sum up the plan of salvation in all of its simplicity.

"A" — "Acknowledge your sin." Admit your guilt, and come to Him without any claim of righteousness or merit of your own, without any dependence upon your own works, goodness, religion, or morality, and acknowledge that without the blood of Christ, you are utterly and eternally lost.

And then the "B" of salvation. "Believe on the Lord Jesus Christ, and thou shalt be saved." It is faith alone that saves, because there is no merit in man's work whatsoever. And finally, "C" — Confess before the Lord, for He Himself has

Chapter Five

THE BLOOD FOUNDATION

THE tabernacle in the wilderness is the only building ever erected having a foundation made of pure silver. The entire building rested on blocks of silver, one hundred in number, each block weighing about one hundred pounds. The total weight of the foundation, therefore, was ten thousand pounds, or five tons. These one hundred sockets, or blocks of silver, were arranged in the shape of a rectangle, forty-five feet long and fifteen feet wide. In each block of silver was a hole into which were fitted the two projections at the base of each upright board which formed the walls of the tabernacle proper. These blocks of silver were placed upon the desert ground, the upright boards were placed on the sockets of silver with their tenons fitting snugly into the foundation stones. These upright boards were then bound together by five gold-plated bars which ran the length of the walls of the building and bound the boards into one rigid whole. The result was an enclosure of upright, gold-plated boards, forty-five feet long, fifteen feet wide, and fifteen feet high. Over this rectangular enclosure were draped four layers of material, one above the other; first a linen sheet, next a blanket of goats' hair cloth; then a blanket of rams' skins, and finally a leather covering made of badger skins.

This little building, the size of an ample living room, rested, therefore, upon a foundation that seemed wholly out of proportion to the building itself. The foundation alone weighed five tons, and was made of solid silver sockets. The tabernacle is a picture, of course, of the Lord Jesus Christ, and also of the believer who is "IN Christ." Everything depends upon this foundation, all of it rests upon this one base. The silver foundation speaks of the blood of the Lord Jesus Christ on which our entire redemption depends and hangs. The silver for this foundation was furnished by the children of Israel who had carried it out of the land of Egypt. It was paid as a redemption tax, a tax upon all of the male adults in the congregation of Israel, which every adult Israelite was to pay.

REDEMPTION PRICE

In Exodus 30 we have the instructions for the procuring of this great amount of silver which was to furnish the foundation for the tabernacle.

> And the Lord spake unto Moses, saying,
>
> When thou takest the sum of the children of Israel after their number, then shall they give every man a ransom for his soul unto the Lord . . .
>
> This they shall give, every one that passeth among them that are numbered, half a shekel after the shekel of the sanctuary . . . an half shekel shall be the offering of the Lord.
>
> The rich shall not give more, and the poor shall not give less than half a shekel, when they give an offering unto the Lord, to make an ATONEMENT for your souls (Exodus 30: 11-13, 15).

Silver is here called "atonement" money, which was required of every single Israelite. None were to be excepted. Failure to furnish the silver meant death and cutting off from the assembly of Israel. The amount, however, which was to be given by each individual was easily within reach of all, the rich and the poor alike. It was a very, very nominal sum, but in the aggregate amounted to the five tons of silver required for the foundation of the tabernacle. It amounted to a half shekel, or less than 35 cents for each individual. Silver in the Bible speaks of atonement, and this atonement is always to be by blood. And so we find that the silver foundation upon which the tabernacle rested signified that it was built upon the atoning blood of a substitute. On this foundation, the blood of atonement, the tabernacle of our redemption is also built. And only those who had furnished the half shekel of silver could be numbered among the children of Israel. Failure to pay the "blood tax" meant certain death.

DAVID'S SON

Many, many years later King David was to be painfully reminded of this lesson, that there can be no numbering of the people without the atonement money. In II Samuel 24 and I Chronicles 21 we have the record of David's great sin. He commanded the people to be numbered, and over the objection of Joab ordered a census; but failure to collect the half shekel of silver resulted in the death of 70,000 of the men of Israel. Only those, therefore, who build on the blood, who claim the atonement, can be numbered with God's people.

Now this silver, collected by Moses from all the adult males in Israel, was melted into one hundred sockets of silver. We have the record in Exodus 38:25, 27:

> And the silver of them that were numbered of the congregation was an hundred talents, and a thousand seven hundred and threescore and fifteen shekels, after the shekel of the sanctuary:
> And of the hundred talents of silver were cast the sockets of the sanctuary, and the sockets of the veil; an hundred sockets of the hundred talents, a talent for a socket.

The tabernacle in Israel, therefore, rested entirely upon a foundation of the silver, the atonement money, collected from the children of Israel. Silver, therefore, becomes in the Bible a symbol and a figure of the price of atonement. As there is no atonement without blood, this silver, therefore, immediately points to the blood, and especially to the blood of the Lord Jesus Christ. In Leviticus 17:11 we read:

> For the life of the flesh is in the blood: and I have given

it to you upon the altar to make an atonement for your souls: for it is the blood that maketh an atonement for the soul.

Silver then is definitely, and beyond a question of doubt, atonement money. Atonement is by the blood, and therefore, the silver in the tabernacle speaks of blood, and the tabernacle rested on this foundation of blood. This silver foundation becomes a symbol, and a most beautiful symbol of the precious blood of the Lord Jesus Christ, which was shed on Calvary's Cross, on which our whole redemption rests and is builded as the only foundation.

Without shedding of blood is no remission (Hebrews 9:22).

Our redemption has been bought with a precious price. It was the price of the blood of the Son of God, for this silver under the tabernacle was merely a type of the blood of our Saviour. Paul tells us:

Ye are bought with a price (I Corinthians 6:20).

Peter tells us:

Ye were not redeemed with corruptible things, as silver and gold . . .

But with the precious blood of Christ, as of a lamb without blemish and without spot (I Peter 1:18, 19).

It is called PRECIOUS blood. It means that it is of tremendous and inestimable worth. It was precious because it was the blood of God, not the blood of a man. Now if that statement seems to be strange and bold, we would remind you that the Bible clearly teaches that it was the "blood of God" which was shed on Calvary. The blood of the Lord Jesus Christ was not derived from man, but it was divine blood, and the divine contribution, the blood of God. Jesus was virgin born, without a human father. The blood in Christ was a divine contribution. Paul settles this beyond all dispute in Acts 20:28, where he says to the Ephesian elders:

Take heed therefore unto yourselves, and to all the flock . . . to feed the church of God, which he hath purchased with his own blood.

Notice the words — "the church of God, which he [God] hath purchased with his own [God's] blood." Since it was the blood of Christ, He must of necessity have been God, because it is called "the blood of God." Jesus is God, and His blood, therefore, was the blood of Almighty God Himself. No wonder that Peter calls it "precious blood."

Everything, therefore, depends upon the blood of Christ because it is divine blood. There is no salvation apart from personal appropriation of that blood by faith. Man may make light of it, and may refuse to accept it, but the fact remains, without the shedding of blood there is no remission, and without the blood of the Lord Jesus Christ there is absolutely no salvation. The natural man, of course, rejects this, and calls our theology a theology of the shambles and the butcher shop, but the fact remains that without this blood there is no approach to God. It is the very foundation, the very rock, the very silver foundation upon which all of our hope is built. If any man build on this foundation, he shall be saved.

> For other foundation can no man lay than that is laid, which is Jesus Christ (I Corinthians 3:11).

Symbol of the Church

The tabernacle is a picture of three things: (1) Christ, (2) salvation, and (3) the Church. For the priest entering into the tabernacle by the blood at the altar, points to the Lord Jesus Christ as he entered the heavenly tabernacle. In Hebrews 9:11 and 12 we read:

> But Christ being come an high priest of good things to come, by a greater and more perfect tabernacle, not made with hands, that is to say, not of this building;
> Neither by the blood of goats and calves, but by his own blood he entered in once into the holy place, having obtained ETERNAL REDEMPTION for us.

The blood of Christ obtained eternal redemption for us. The services in the tabernacle needed to be repeated continually, from day to day, and from year to year.

> For it is not possible that the blood of bulls and of goats should take away sins.
>
> And every priest standeth daily ministering and offering oftentimes the same sacrifices, which can never take away sins:
>
> But this man, after he had offered one sacrifice for sins for ever, sat down on the right hand of God;
>
> For by one offering he hath perfected for ever them that are sanctified (Hebrews 10:4, 11, 12, 14).

In conclusion we want to gather up the teaching of this important fact of the silver foundation of the tabernacle. Remember that it rested upon the atonement money received from the children of Israel. This was a shadow of the price of redemption, the blood of the Lord Jesus Christ. But this atonement of one half shekel, thirty-five cents, must be individually given. Every man had to bring his own half shekel. The rich and the poor alike, without difference, must bring their bit of silver. It was an individual responsibility. And salvation, beloved, is also a personal, individual matter, and can never be obtained by proxy. You are not saved by the religion of your parents, or because someone had you baptized or because you joined the church, or lived a good life, or are religious in your activities. It must be by a personal act of faith in the death, the resurrection, and the blood of the Lord Jesus Christ, so that you, too, can say from the heart, and not only sing with your lips:

> My hope is built on nothing less,
> Than Jesus' blood and righteousness.
> I dare not trust the sweetest frame,
> But only lean on Jesus' Name.
>
> On Christ, and on His Blood I stand,
> All other ground is sinking sand.

The entire thing becomes a personal responsibility. You cannot be saved by the religion of your parents, or by anything that any other human has done, but only by a personal faith in the work of the Lord Jesus Christ. Have you ever, as a poor lost sinner, realizing your absolute inability to do anything to obtain your salvation, come to the Cross of Christ, realizing that He had to die because of your absolute inability to do anything for yourself, and thus be saved? May God grant you grace to receive Him now,

For whosoever shall call upon the name of the Lord shall be saved (Romans 10:13).

Chapter Six

THE ROOF OF THE TABERNACLE

THE tabernacle in the wilderness rested upon a foundation of one hundred silver sockets weighing one hundred pounds each. Upon this foundation stood forty-eight upright boards made of acacia wood, and covered with pure gold. Each board was fifteen feet long, and over two feet wide. These boards had two projections on the lower end, and these projections fit into the silver foundation sockets. The upright boards were then held together by five horizontal bars of gold-covered wood. We come now to the roof of the tabernacle, the shelter under which the priest was to minister in the sanctuary.

Four Layers

The roof of the tabernacle consisted of four layers of material. The first covering placed over the tabernacle, and, therefore, the only one which would be visible from the inside, was a curtain of fine twined linen, embroidered with blue and purple and scarlet color. It covered the entire top of the tabernacle and hung over the sides, almost to the ground. Beautifully embroidered in the pattern of this linen sheet were the figures of cherubim overshadowing both the holy place, and the holy of holies. This main curtain consisted of ten separate curtains coupled together to make one great covering for the interior of the tabernacle. Moses received minute instructions as recorded in Exodus 26:1,

> Moreover thou shalt make the tabernacle with ten curtains of fine twined linen, and blue, and purple, and scarlet: with cherubims of cunning work shalt thou make them.

This beautiful curtain formed the ceiling of the tabernacle proper, visible only and exclusively from the inside, visible only to the worshiper who had by way of the altar and the laver been admitted into the sanctuary itself. The outsider, on the outside of the tabernacle, saw nothing of its exquisite beauty. All he was able to see was the drab leather covering of badger skins, unattractive, somber, and unappealing to the natural eye.

The linen curtain which formed the ceiling represents Christ in all the glory of His perfect righteousness and redemptive work. The outside badger skins were Christ in His humiliation, in His humanity, and in His suffering upon the Cross of Calvary. To see Christ as the Son of God, the glorious Redeemer, we must see Him from within. We must be IN CHRIST to know the beauty of Christ; and the only way, of course, to be IN CHRIST is to come through the door, by way of the blood.

Now the curtain which formed the ceiling of the tabernacle was in four colors, blue, scarlet, purple and white. Blue stands for Christ's heavenly origin; scarlet for His sacrificial death; purple for His royal character and His regal nature; and white, His sinless righteousness and perfection.

In addition there were cherubim with outstretched wings hovering as it were over the priest in the sanctuary, watching every move he made. Cherubim in the Bible are guardians of the holiness of God. They are holy ones who are the attendants of the throne of God, and their song is given to us as "Holy, Holy, Holy, Lord God Almighty." Ezekiel tells us the cherubim were living creatures, which had four faces, the face of a man, a lion, an ox, and an eagle.

And in all of this we have a picture of the fourfold character of the person of the Lord Jesus Christ, who, of course, is set forth by the shadow of the entire tabernacle in all of its detailed structure.

The face of a man speaks of His perfect humanity; the lion speaks of His kingship and power; the ox is the symbol of sacrifice and service; and the eagle of the ability to see great distances, and therefore speaks of omniscience. All of this the believer sees in the Lord Jesus Christ, once he has entered by faith into Christ, and into the more perfect tabernacle by way of the altar and by way of the blood. To the outsider, all this glory is completely hidden, and he cannot comprehend how we can become so enamored and enraptured and infatuated with the loveliness of the all-sufficient beauty of our Lord and Saviour Jesus Christ.

Goats' Hair Curtains

The second layer of the roof of the tabernacle was made of goats' hair.

> And thou shalt make curtains of goats' hair to be a covering upon the tabernacle: eleven curtains shalt thou make (Exodus 26:7).

These goats' hair curtains were placed over the linen curtains, and extended down the sides and back of the tabernacle entirely to the ground. A goat in the Bible is a picture of Christ as our sin-bearer. The goat was a clean animal, fit for sacrifice upon the altar of burnt offering. On the day of atonement, the priest was to take two goats. One was slain at the altar and his blood poured out at the base of the altar, symbolic of the sacrifice of the Lord Jesus Christ in His death.

> And he shall sprinkle of the blood [of the goat] upon it with his finger seven times, and cleanse it, and hallow it from the uncleanness of the children of Israel.
> And when he hath made an end of reconciling the holy place, and the tabernacle of the congregation, and the altar, he shall bring the live goat:
> And Aaron shall lay both his hands upon the head of the live goat, and confess over him all the iniquities of the children of Israel, and all their transgressions in all their sins, putting them upon the head of the goat, and shall send him away by the hand of a fit man into the wilderness:

And the goat shall bear upon him all their iniquities unto a land not inhabited: and he shall let go the goat in the wilderness (Leviticus 16:19-22).

What a tremendous and inexhaustible picture of the Lord Jesus Christ in our place as the sin-bearer all of this presents to us. Our sins were laid upon the Lord Jesus Christ. There was a transference of our guilt to Him, and He paid the price of death by shedding His blood. He took our sins, in order that we might become the recipients of His righteousness. This is taught by the death of the first goat which was to be slain on the day of atonement at the door of the tabernacle. And then the live goat, after having the sins of the people transferred upon him, by confession and the laying on of hands of the priest, is sent into a desert land, never, never to return. It tells us how Christ as our sin-bearer carried our sins, on the basis of the death of the first slain goat, and removed them as far as the east is from the west. Of all this the goats' hair curtains upon the tabernacle speak in great detail. It is Christ our sin-bearer, our Substitute.

The white linen curtains of which we have spoken, and which formed the ceiling of the tabernacle proper, of course, were underneath these goats' hair curtains, indicating that our acceptance in Christ and our righteousness and salvation depend upon the substitutionary work of our sin-bearer, the Lord Jesus Christ Himself. What terrible blasphemy, therefore, it is to teach (as some do) that the second goat represents Satan, and the Devil is the scapegoat who will have all our sins laid upon him and bear them forever and ever. What blasphemy, we repeat, for the Bible is clear that:

The Lord hath laid on HIM the iniquity of us all (Isaiah 53:6).

Christ was once offered to bear the sins of many (Hebrews 9:28).

He hath made HIM to be sin for us, who knew no sin (II Corinthians 5:21).

All of this, therefore, is suggested by the curtains of goats'
hair as the second covering of the tabernacle. Christ "bare
our sins in His own body on the tree." Yea, more, He
"became sin for us." This fact was the reason for the agony
of Calvary and Gethsemane. Jesus did not shrink from suffering, He did not dread the Cross, He did not fear death,
for He had said of His life:

> No man taketh it from me, but I lay it down of myself. I
> have power to lay it down, and I have power to take it again
> (John 10:18).

Our Lord Jesus Christ feared nothing except sin: s-i-n!
It was when the Father offered Him the cup of sin in Gethsemane, that He cried, "Oh, my Father, if it be possible,
let THIS cup pass from me." And in this cup were all the
dregs of humanity's sin and iniquity and corruption. As
He looked into its limpid, putrid depths, and caught the
stench of humanity's sin, His holy soul shrank from the
only thing Christ ever feared, SIN, and He cried out as He
looked into that cup:

> My Father, if it be possible, let this cup pass from me.

But for the love He had for us, He did take the cup.
He took our sin, our guilt, and our iniquity to Calvary,
and there reached the acme of sin's penalty, to be forsaken
of Almighty God Himself. As God looked upon the Lord
Jesus Christ, He saw our sin, which Christ had assumed —
my sin and your sin — and a holy God, who cannot look
upon sin, saw this terrible thing upon His own Son, and
therefore turned His back upon His only Son, the Son of
God, snuffed out the lights of heaven, pulled down the
shades of the sky in eternal darkness about His Son, until
in the utter desperate agony of His soul, His Son cried:

> My God, my God, why hast thou forsaken me?

Of course, we know the answer to this question of the
Lord Jesus Christ. It was sin, nothing else but sin, s-i-n.
Jesus bore our sin there as our sin-bearer on the Cross, but

He bore it, He paid the price, and like the slain goat, made atonement, and like the live goat, carried our sins away, and cast them forever into the depths of the sea, and now we can sing:

> Gone, gone, gone, gone, Yes, my sins are gone.
> Buried in the depths of the deepest sea,
> Yes, my sins are gone.

This we believe to be the lesson of the goats' hair covering, which was above the linen covering. It speaks of our complete salvation, and our perfect righteousness in the Lord Jesus Christ. In our coming message we shall take up the tremendously significant symbolism and typology of the other two coverings of the tabernacle.

In conclusion, however, a very important thought. The one goat slain at the hands of the priest could not avail by itself. The offerer must place both hands upon the head of the live goat, and confess over him his sins. Notice, therefore, that on the day of atonement, great picture of the work of the Lord Jesus Christ on the Cross of Calvary, there is both death, and there is life. There is a slain goat, and there is a goat which is not slain. The slain goat is God's part in our redemption. The live goat brings us face to face with man's part — personal appropriation. The slain goat speaks of the death of the Lord Jesus Christ upon the Cross of Calvary; the live goat speaks of His living today, having borne our sins, and made complete reconciliation for us. But we must remember, the priest was to lay his hand of faith, confession and repentance upon the head of the goat, and then send it away into the wilderness. In Leviticus 16:20-21 we read:

> . . . he shall bring the live goat:
> And Aaron shall lay both his hands upon the head of the live goat, and confess over him all the iniquities of the children of Israel.

When the Lord Jesus Christ died on the Cross of Calvary, and rose again the third day, God exhausted heaven in His effort to make possible salvation for men and women. God Himself can do no more for the sinner who refuses to receive God's provision. To refuse to accept is to make it as though the Lord Jesus Christ had never been born or died, or had been raised from the dead. It avails only to those who will place the hands of confession and repentance and faith on the head of the sacrifice, and accept Him as Substitute, and then go on to serve Him as Lord and Master of their lives. Have you, my friend, ever done this? Have you ever seen yourself in the sight of God as utterly unworthy, only worthy of death, and by faith in the finished work and the shed blood of Jesus Christ, placed your faith in Him, and been saved according to the promise of God:

Believe on the Lord Jesus Christ, and thou shalt be saved (Acts 16:31).

Chapter Seven

BADGER SKINS AND SHOES

THE roof of the tabernacle in the wilderness consisted of four consecutive layers of cloth and weather-proof leather. The innermost layer forming the decorated ceiling of the tabernacle was of the finest white linen embroidered in blue and red and purple, and decorated with the figures of cherubim with outstretched wings, looking down as it were upon those who worshiped in the tabernacle. The next layer above this linen layer was made of goats' hair. The linen curtain was symbolic of Christ's resurrection glory; it was covered by the goats' hair curtain, symbolic of the sin offering made by Christ upon the Cross. There can be no righteousness and resurrection glory without the Cross of Calvary, and so the goats' hair curtains are superimposed upon the white linen curtains in the forming of the ceiling of the tabernacle. We come now to the third and fourth layers from the inside to the outside of the roof.

> And thou shalt make a covering for the tent of rams' skins dyed red, and a covering above of badgers' skins (Exodus 26:14).

The third layer forming the roof of the tabernacle was made of leather, rams' skins tanned and dyed a deep crimson red color, and coupled together to make one large covering which was placed over the lower two coverings of the linen and goats' hair curtains.

RAM AS SUBSTITUTE

The rams' skins pointed to the Lord Jesus Christ in the role of a Substitute for sinners. It speaks of the substitutionary atonement made by the blood of the Lord Jesus Christ in our behalf. The color, red, as it occurs in the tabernacle, invariably speaks of the blood of the Lord Jesus Christ and the atonement which He made for sins. The skins, of course, speak of the complete covering for the sinner who dwells underneath this canopy.

The first mention of skins is in Genesis 3:21. You will recall that Adam had sinned and broken with his God by partaking of the forbidden fruit. In his blind, sinful depravity, he had sewed fig leaves together in a flimsy apron, in a vain effort to cover his sin by the work of his own hands. But the Lord would not accept Adam's fig leaf garments, and utterly rejected them. Instead, the Lord now slew an animal (probably a ram), poured out its blood, and from its skin made a coat for Adam and for Eve, our first parents. The lesson, of course, in this first recorded sacrifice, is plain. The first record of death and its implications is definitely made clear by the Lord. Adam was under the sentence of death, and must die for his sin, unless a substitute could be provided. The animal from which God took the skin to clothe Adam was, therefore, a substitute for Adam — it took Adam's place, and it died Adam's death. The substitute must die, the substitute must give its blood, before the sinner can be clothed by the covering of the skin of this substitute. This is the lesson of God's plan of substitutionary atonement laid down at the very dawn of creation, and there has never been any departure or deviation from this rule.

It became a fixed rule for all acceptable, substitutionary sacrifices thereafter. There was to be no deviation from this God-given plan. Cain tried it, and failed. He brought of the best of the fruit of the ground to God for an offering, in all sincerity and religious piety, but God refused his attempt to cover himself once again with fig leaves of his own manufacture, because without death and the shedding of blood there can be no substitution.

On the other hand, Abel brought a ram, a firstling of the flock. He killed it; he shed its blood; and God accepted it in the place of Abel, and showed His acceptance by causing fire to fall from heaven and consume the sacrifice upon the altar. You will notice that the ram took Abel's place in substitution, and the blood made an atonement for his sins. Two thousand years later it was still the same. The ram was still a type of our Substitute, the Lord Jesus Christ, and when He came, He was the fulfillment, not only of the substitute which God provided for Adam and Eve, but also the one which Abel presented in faith before the Lord.

ABRAHAM AND ISAAC

In Genesis 22 we have another illustration of this same truth. Abraham is told to take Isaac, his son, to Mt. Moriah, to be sacrificed upon an altar. But Isaac himself was a sinner and needed someone to atone for his sins, and so after Abraham had laid Isaac on the altar and lifted the knife to slay his son, he was suddenly arrested and interrupted by God, who ordered him to stay his hand; and Abraham, turning from the altar,

> lifted up his eyes, and looked, and behold behind him a RAM caught in a thicket by his horns (Genesis 22:13).

Here again we come face to face with God's "ram." Here was God's provision for Isaac who too was a sinner. Isaac was under the sentence of death, and deserved to die. God's justice demanded that he should die. The law demanded that he should die. The hand of judgment was poised, and then suddenly the ram appears and Isaac is spared, and we read on in Genesis 22:13,

> And Abraham went and took the ram, and offered him up for a burnt offering IN THE STEAD OF HIS SON (Genesis 22:13).

Notice carefully those words, IN THE STEAD OF HIS SON:

that is, IN THE PLACE OF HIS SON. And Abraham realized that it was a picture of the coming substitute, the Lord Jesus Christ. How clearly Abraham realized this we do not know, but he certainly did have a faint inkling of its prophetic implications, for we read in Genesis 22:14,

> And Abraham called the name of that place Jehovah-jireh [Jehovah will provide a substitute for me]: as it is said to this day, In the mount of the Lord [Mt. Calvary] it shall be seen.

Nineteen hundred years ago all of these types were completely fulfilled in the person of the Lord Jesus Christ. He came to cover the sinner with His own blood, just as the priest in the tabernacle was sheltered under the rams' skin, the leather scarlet-red curtain overhead. The ram, therefore, is a symbol of the substitution of God for the sinner.

The Lord Jesus Christ came into the world to be a substitute for guilty sinners. He came to take the place of condemned men and women. He came to exchange places with those who were under the sentence of death. He took the sinner's place upon the Cross of Calvary, that the believing sinner might take his place in the Father's house. In Luke 10 we have another picture of substitution. The good Samaritan, you will remember, in his search for wounded men, came upon the man beaten by thugs, stripped, and left half dead. We read of him:

> But a certain Samaritan, as he journeyed, came where he was (Luke 10:33).

Notice the words carefully, "came where he was." It is a picture of the Lord Jesus Christ, the Good Samaritan, the Great Physician, leaving the glory of His Father's house to come into this world, down, down, down, to where we were on the way to hell and destruction. He came and took our nature, our humanity, He stooped to the depths where we lay wounded and half dead. He became like unto us in all things, sin only excepted. He came where we were. We read further:

And went to him, and bound up his wounds, pouring in oil and wine, and SET HIM ON HIS OWN BEAST (Luke 10:34).

Again notice the words, "set him on his own beast." Here is complete change of places, perfect substitution. He took the poor, wounded man's place in the dust and then exalted him to his place upon his own beast. This is an illustration of what we mean by substitution, and this is the message of the rams' skins dyed red, covering the tabernacle, and sheltering the ministering priests under the atoning blood, and making him secure under the blood.

BADGERS' SKINS

We come now, finally, to the fourth and outer covering of the tabernacle. The record is very brief:

And thou shalt make a covering for the tent [tabernacle] of rams' skins dyed red, and a covering above of badgers' skins (Exodus 26:14).

These badgers' skins had no colorful beauty; they were drab, dull and bluish grey. The outer covering was exposed to the sun and the rain and the storm and the elements continually. It was the only covering visible to the outsider, and had nothing appealing about it at all. It gave little hint of the beauty beneath the drab exterior.

All of this, of course, is a perfect picture of the humanity of the Lord Jesus Christ, and that which alone is visible to the outsider before he enters in at the Door. This is all that the world, the unbeliever, the unregenerate man can possibly see of the Lord Jesus Christ. There is no attractiveness about Him. Only those who pass through the door and by the altar, and into the tabernacle itself can behold the breath-taking, exquisite, indescribable beauty inside. But the man on the outside sees only a rectangular building, draped under a coarse, dull leather covering, which held no attraction. It is the picture of our Lord Jesus Christ in His humanity as He walked here upon the earth, as the Sin-bearer of men, His deity veiled by His humanity. Isaiah said of Jesus, as symbolized by these badgers' skins:

> He hath no form nor comeliness; and when we shall see him, there is no beauty that we should desire him.
>
> He is despised and rejected of men; a man of sorrows, and acquainted with grief: and we hid as it were our faces from him; he was despised, and we esteemed him not (Isaiah 53:2-3).

The badgers' skins, then, represent all that the world can see in the person of the Lord Jesus Christ, until they have been born again. They are still on the outside where the winds tear, the rain pelts, the sun bakes, and the frost bites. It is the exposed portion of the tabernacle which they are able to see, and that portion is a fit figure of our Lord's human body, in which He bore our sins on the tree. It was in this body that the storms of human hate placed a crown of thorns upon His head. It was this body upon which they spit, which they struck, and slapped and scourged. In this body He was exposed to all the ignominy of the Cross and the storms of human hate; the nails pierced His hands and feet, and the blood gushed forth. This is the meaning of the badgers' skins.

PORPOISE LEATHER

The word "badger" in the original is "porpoise." This outer covering of skins was made of leather, and the skins were taken from porpoises — not badgers as it is in our English translation. The porpoise was a marine animal, a sea animal which teemed abundantly in the Nile and the Red Sea. It is related to the whale and the dolphin. Its hide made excellent leather. Israel had no trouble obtaining porpoise leather from the abundant waters while they were in Egypt, but here in the desert, far from the sea, they could not obtain them. Evidently the Israelites had stocked up on these leather skins when they left the land of Egypt, and for a very good reason, for they were to pass through a rough and a howling desert, and the porpoise leather was the material from which their shoes were made, and utterly unobtainable in the desert.

LEATHER SHOES

In Ezekiel 16:10 we read the use to which this porpoise leather was usually put. Here we have a bit of information which is exceedingly interesting in the light of our study of the tabernacle:

> I clothed thee also with broidered work, and SHOD THEE WITH BADGERS' SKIN (Ezekiel 16:10).

Notice the words, "I shod thee with porpoise skins." This leather was for shoe leather, and now the Lord demands that they give this precious leather, plentiful in Egypt, but unobtainable in the desert, for the covering of the tabernacle in the service of God. God asked them to give up their shoe leather — literally give the shoes off their feet — for the service of God. It seems like an unreasonable demand, superficially observed. We can imagine Israel saying, "But Lord, we need this leather for our shoes. We are in a rough, rocky wilderness, and shoes soon wear out, and if we give you our shoe leather, we will soon be barefooted, and unable to proceed over these rocks. If we give these porpoise skins reserved for our shoe leather, what shall we do for shoes?"

And the Lord seems to say, "I thought of that, too. I thought of all that beforehand, and made provision for it. You give me all your shoe leather, and I'll take care of your feet. I'll give you something better and more wonderful than new shoes. I'll give you shoes that won't wear out." And the glorious record of the Bible is that God did take care of Israel's feet. In Deuteronomy 8:4 we read:

> Thy raiment waxed not old upon thee, neither did thy foot swell.

In Deuteronomy 29:5 the Lord says:

> And I have led you forty years in the wilderness: your clothes are not waxen old upon you, and thy shoe is not waxen old upon thy foot.

And Nehemiah too was impressed by the provision, for we read in Nehemiah 9:21,

> Yea, forty years didst thou sustain them in the wilderness, so that they lacked nothing; their clothes waxed not old, and their feet swelled not.

God seems to say, "Give me your shoe leather, and I will take care of your feet, from here on in." Israel trusted God, and was not disappointed, for the Israelites went for forty years, while their clothes waxed not old and their shoes did not wear out. Oh, for a faith like that in these days, as we pass through the wilderness of this world, filled with animosity and resistance to the Gospel of Jesus Christ. It is the path of victory. If we are willing to turn over everything to His care, and trust Him completely, He will never fail us, but be with us according to His promise, "even unto the end of the age." I think it fitting to close with the words of the Apostle Paul, as we think of the faith of Israel in giving their shoe leather for the service of the Lord, when he says to us in Philippians:

> Be careful for nothing; but in everything by prayer and supplication with thanksgiving let your requests be made known unto God.

> And the peace of God, which passeth all understanding, shall keep your hearts and minds through Christ Jesus (Philippians 4: 6-7).

Chapter Eight

ROPES AND PINS

. . . all the pins of the court, shall be of brass (Exodus 27:19b).
The pins of the tabernacle, and the pins of the court, and their cords (Exodus 35:18).

THE tabernacle in the wilderness, though portable and constructed without nails, screws, hinges, or glue, was a structure so sturdy that it withstood the howling storms of the wilderness for forty long years. The winds blew upon it, the storms swept over it, the rains beat upon it, but it could not be moved. The most secure place in all the camp of Israel was in the tabernacle, and we believe that this is what David sings of when he says:

He that dwelleth in the secret place of the most High shall abide under the shadow of the Almighty.

I will say of the Lord, He is my refuge and my fortress: my God; in him will I trust.

A thousand shall fall at thy side, and ten thousand at thy right hand; but it shall not come nigh thee.

Because thou hast made the Lord, which is my refuge, even the most High, thy habitation (Psalm 91:1, 2, 7, 9).

David was undoubtedly thinking of the priest as he served in the tabernacle in the wilderness. The free rendering of this verse might well be read as follows:

He that dwelleth in the holy place of the most High shall abide under the wings of the cherubim.

In the holy place of God's tabernacle, under the overshadowing figures of the cherubim with outstretched wings, under the blood, the priest was safe and secure from every ill and danger. The tabernacle, of course, is Christ. We

63

have already established this definitely in the Book of Hebrews. The priest in the tabernacle becomes a figure of the believer who is IN the Lord Jesus Christ, and those who are in the Lord Jesus Christ are forever safe and eternally secure. Nothing can reach them there. This security of the tabernacle was due to its sturdy construction, its secure foundation, all of which pointed forward to the person of the Lord Jesus Christ. You will recall that this tabernacle was built upon a foundation of solid silver. The boards and the walls were securely and deeply mortised into the silver sockets, and bound together with golden bars. Over it all was a four-ply roof, impervious to wind and rain, absolutely weatherproof and rainproof.

THE PINS AND THE CORDS

But it was still further made secure by a large number of tent pins driven deeply into the ground all around the tabernacle proper. Ropes were passed tightly over the roof of badgers' skins, and secured to the pins on each side and back of the tabernacle. These ropes, attached to the tent pins in the ground, made the entire structure absolutely rigid and secure. During the entire forty years of its use it was never shaken, though the desert storms must have beaten mercilessly upon it. There is no record that it ever moved a fraction of an inch. The priest, therefore, inside the tabernacle was absolutely secure because the tabernacle itself was secure. The believer in Christ (the New Testament priest) is also secure. He is as secure as Christ Himself, for he is IN CHRIST.

REASON FOR SECURITY

Now these tent pins are also called "nails" in the Bible. In other places they are called "stakes." In Isaiah 22:23-24, in a direct reference, Christ is compared to a "nail":

> And I will fasten him as a nail in a sure place; and he shall be for a glorious throne to his father's house.

And they shall hang upon him all the glory of his father's house.

The pins or nails, therefore, point to the Lord Jesus Christ in securing the believer in Himself. These pins were made of brass, resistant to rust and corrosion, not affected by the elements of the desert. They speak of the incorruptible life and death of our Lord Jesus in bearing the judgment of Almighty God for our sins. These pins, these brass pins, were buried deeply into the ground, with the upper parts of them above the ground, and here we have the ground of our entire security in the Gospel of the Lord Jesus Christ. We repeat, the pins were buried in the ground, but also emerged from the ground, and it speaks of the death and the resurrection, that which is buried, and that which is above the ground. The part of the pins beneath the ground becomes a symbol of the death of the Lord Jesus Christ; the part above the ground suggests His resurrection. And this is the Gospel, the "good news" of salvation, the finished work which makes us secure. If the pins were driven all the way into the ground, they would be worthless. Part of them must be above the ground in order that the ropes may be attached to them. So, too, the death of the Lord Jesus Christ by itself could not save a single sinner. The good news of the Gospel is not only the Cross, not only the death of Christ for sinners, but it is the death *plus* the resurrection of our Saviour. The pins are buried, but also rise above the ground in order to make us secure.

DEATH INSUFFICIENT

If, therefore, the Lord Jesus Christ had merely died, and remained in the tomb, even though He had paid for all our sins, all of it would have been in vain, for death is the penalty for sin. If one single sin had remained unpaid for by the Lord Jesus Christ, He would still be holden in the bonds of death. Remember, the "wages of *sin* is death." One sin will bring on eternal death. It does not say, "the wages of *sins*," but *"sin."* One single sin means death. It was for one single sin that God cursed Adam and all humanity and all creation in the Garden of Eden. There are no "little" sins. All sin is a great thing in God's sight. We speak of little sins, but with Him there are no little sins. We have but to think of our parents' first sin. It was in human estimation a little thing, just taking a fruit from a forbidden tree. We would call it no more than petty larceny. No judge would condemn a man to death for picking an apple from a neighbor's tree. But God did! Yes, God did! For He plunged the entire race into death because of that *one* sin. The "wages of *sin* is death."

THE RESURRECTION

The resurrection of the Lord Jesus Christ, therefore, meant that every sin had been successfully paid for. Not a single sin remained unatoned. Had Jesus paid for all the sins of mankind except *one,* He would have still remained in death and be there today. His resurrection, therefore, is the proof that when Jesus cried, "It is finished," it was indeed finished, and His resurrection proved this to all of the world, to all generations, and now the only sin which can condemn a man today is refusal to accept as a free gift this finished salvation. Yes, the pins which make us secure were buried in the ground, but they also rose above the ground. It is faith in a resurrected Christ which alone can save. Faith in Jesus as a good Man, a noble Example, a great Teacher, and a Reformer and Martyr who died for a noble cause, and for others, all this will not save a single soul. It must be faith in a crucified, risen, resurrected Lord, a Saviour who is truly God, for only God could bear away the sins of the entire world and yet arise from the dead.

All of this is taught, therefore, by the brazen stakes of the tabernacle, and to these were attached the ropes which held down and made the building secure. But remember that the ropes or cords were tied, not to the part of the stakes which was buried, but to the part which rose above the ground. The upper part is the resurrected Christ, and we can place our hope only in a living, resurrected Lord, who indeed died and was buried, but who also arose and lives today.

THE CORDS

Before concluding this chapter, however, we must add just a word about the ropes which passed over the tabernacle, and were secured to the pins of brass. These are called in the Scripture "cords." These cords or ropes, held the tabernacle firmly together, and made it indestructible. The cords speak of the love of Christ as being the only hope of the redeemed sinner. Hosea records Jehovah as speaking to Israel:

> I drew them with cords of a man, with bands of love (Hosea 11:4).

We are, therefore, made secure in Christ by the cords of His infinite love. These cords were attached to the brazen pins. The love of Christ is seen, therefore, in His death and resurrection, as exemplified by these brazen pins driven into the ground, and yet emerging from the ground. This is the great evidence of His love. It is the demonstration of the infinite love of Christ for us. Speaking of mere human love Jesus said,

> Greater love hath no man than this, that a man lay down his life for his friends (John 15:13).

Of course, that is mere human love. It is the acme of mere human love. Beyond this, human love cannot rise. As a father I could willingly die for Mrs. De Haan and my children. I could die for my grandchildren. Some would die for a dear friend, or a helpless child, but that is the limit of human love. It is natural to hate our enemies, and love only those who love us. But divine love transcends all this, for listen to Paul in Romans 5:6 and 7:

>For when we were yet without strength, in due time Christ died for the UNGODLY.

>For scarcely for a righteous man will one die: yet peradventure for a good man some would even dare to die.

Now that is the limit of human love, "for a good man some would even dare to die." But now listen to this:

>But God commendeth his love toward us, in that, while we were yet sinners, Christ died for us (Romans 5:8).

God's love for sinners — oh, the wonder of it all! — that He would love the unloving and the unlovable, and the unlovely. Behold the love of Christ on Calvary! See Him hanging, beaten, bound, bleeding, suffering, with cruel nails in His hands and feet, the spittle upon His face, a crown of thorns upon His brow, and yet He was God, and He did not need to suffer thus. Why did He not come down, and deliver Himself, and let us go to our destiny, which would have been our just desert and no one could have lifted a finger of objection to Him. It was just because of the love of God — the love of God in the Lord Jesus Christ. We shall never tire of quoting John 3:16,

>For God so loved the world, that he gave his only begotten Son, that whosoever believeth in him should not perish, but have everlasting life.

We have then, in the pins of the tabernacle, the Lord Jesus Christ fulfilling the demands of a righteous God and a broken law, that by His death and resurrection He should be able to save those to the uttermost who come by faith to Him. But then to this Gospel is attached the love of God which holds us firm in His own keeping. We are bound to God by the cords of love, which, indeed, are absolutely unbreakable.

>I've found a Friend, oh, such a Friend;
> He loved me ere I knew Him!
>He drew me with the cords of love,
> And thus He bound me to Him.

And I give unto them eternal life; and they shall never perish, neither shall any man pluck them out of my hand (John 10:28).

Chapter Nine

THE SHADOW OF THE CROSS

And thou shalt make an altar of shittim wood, five cubits long, and five cubits broad; the altar shall be foursquare: and the height thereof shall be three cubits.

Hollow with boards shalt thou make it: as it was shewed thee in the mount, so shall they make it (Exodus 27:1, 8).

THE first article of furniture the sinner passing through the eastern gate of the tabernacle encountered, was the altar of burnt offering. The word "altar" signifies "to lift up." The altar, the place of lifting up, points to the Cross of the Lord Jesus Christ, of which He Himself said:

And I, if I be lifted up from the earth, will draw all men unto me (John 12:32).

This altar was the place of substitutionary sacrifice. The blood of the animal was poured out at the base of the altar, and the body was consumed upon the altar itself. It was the place of death. It stood between the gate of the court and the approach to the tabernacle. It barred the way to everyone who would come. There was no approach to the tabernacle except by way of this altar, which, of course, speaks of the Cross of the Lord Jesus Christ, and also bars the way of every sinner coming to God. Until he stops at this altar and appropriates the blood, and accepts the sacrifice as a substitute, there is no further progress. It was both a way to God, and a barrier to God. If the Israelite brought his offering to the priest, and it was offered on the altar, then he could freely approach into the presence of God. If he, however, sought to approach God except by the death of a substitute and by way of the altar, it barred the way completely. There was no other way into the presence of God.

There is no approach to God except by the Cross of the Lord Jesus Christ, and by faith in His death and substitutionary sacrifice. The Israelite might bring the most beautiful, perfect, lovely, spotless lamb to the priest, but unless it was killed and offered as a sacrifice in the place of the sinner, it availed absolutely nothing at all. We too may extol the perfections of the Lord Jesus Christ, admire His sinless beauty, sing of His virtues, magnify His graciousness and laud Him as a perfect example and a noble martyr to a noble cause, but it will not do without His death, and personal faith in His shed blood. The death of the Lord Jesus Christ on the Cross, therefore, not His life, is our only hope of salvation. The Cross stands squarely between the sinner and God.

God's Pattern

This altar of burnt offering was made by man, but designed by Almighty God in heaven itself. It was according to the pattern shown to Moses in the Mount. Again and again this direction is given: "See that thou make it according to the pattern which was shown thee in the Mount." When completed, it was God who ignited the wood upon the altar by fire which fell directly from heaven. Man's part in the death of Christ was making the Cross, and placing the sacrifice upon it, and there his part ceased entirely. That is all the sinner can do. By the hands of men, therefore, Jesus was bound and led to Calvary, and impaled upon the Cross, but they could do this only because it was according to the plan and purpose and pattern which God had given beforehand. This death of the Lord Jesus Christ upon the Cross, therefore, was no accident. It was no surprise to God, but planned by Him from eternity. Jesus Himself says:

> For God so loved the world, that HE GAVE his only be-
> gotten Son, that whosoever believeth in him should not perish,
> but have everlasting life (John 3:16).

And Peter says in Acts that Jesus,

> being delivered by the determinate counsel and foreknowledge
> of God, ye have taken, and by wicked hands have crucified
> and slain (Acts 2:23).

Man could not have touched the Lord Jesus Christ or
done anything to Him at all, except according to the pattern
and purpose and permission of Almighty God, and the fact
that Jesus voluntarily gave Himself into the hands of sinners
to be slain. Jesus was not overpowered and led to the Cross
involuntarily, but gave Himself willingly to be

> brought as a lamb to the slaughter, and as a sheep before
> her shearers is dumb, so he openeth not his mouth (Isaiah
> 53:7).

The death of the Lord Jesus Christ, therefore, was entirely voluntary, and so the writer of Hebrews says of Him:

> Once in the end of the world hath he appeared to put away
> sin by the sacrifice of HIMSELF (Hebrews 9:26).

What unfathomable depths of love are seen at this altar
as foreshadowing the Cross of Christ. It was the sins of
Israel which demanded the death of the animal, but it was
by that very death that their sins were atoned for. At Calvary we murdered the Son of God with cruel hands, but
God had planned beforehand that by the murder of His
Son, the murderers themselves might be reconciled to God.
God was able to permit man to kill His Son, Jesus Christ,
on the Cross, in order that by the murder of His Son at
the hands of man, He might save the murderers and reconcile them unto Himself. Surely these are unfathomable
truths, and depths of wisdom which man cannot begin to
understand. Who can fathom the infinite, inscrutable, in-
comprehensible wisdom of God at the altar of burnt offering,
the shadow of the Cross of Christ. We can only stand with
Paul and cry out:

O the depth of the riches both of the wisdom and knowledge of God! how unsearchable are his judgments, and his
ways past finding out! (Romans 11:33).

THE FOUR HORNS

This altar of burnt offering which stood in the court of
the tabernacle had four horns of brass, mounted on the four
corners of the altar. Horns in Scripture are symbolic of great
power. Again and again horns are used as the symbol of
power and might. The Gospel of the Cross is the most
powerful thing in all of existence. Paul says in Romans
1:16 that the Gospel of Christ is

the power of God unto salvation to every one that believeth.

The word "power" in the Greek here is "dynamos," and
means "unlimited power," and is the word from which our
word "dynamite" is derived.

Paul says in I Corinthians 1:18,

For the preaching of the cross is to them that perish fool-
ishness; but unto us which are saved it is the POWER of God.

These horns were mounted upon the four corners of the
altar of burnt offering. They pointed in the four directions
of the compass, North, East, West and South. Now the
first letters of the four directions are "N" for North, "E"
for East, "W" for West, and "S" for South, and the message
of the Cross truly is good "news," N-E-W-S, for all men, north
and east and west and south. It is the good news that Jesus
died and rose again in order to make reconciliation for
sinners with God.

TWO STAVES

The altar in the tabernacle in the wilderness was portable,
made to be carried about from place to place. It was a
provision for a nomad people, who were still in the wilderness, and had not yet been settled in the land of Canaan.
It was, therefore, a provision for pilgrims while they were
passing through the wilderness and therefore was supplied
with two staves by which the priests were able to carry the

altar whenever the order of the Lord caused them to move on.

> And thou shalt make staves for the altar . . .
> And the staves shall be put into the rings, and the staves shall be upon the two sides of the altar, TO BEAR IT (Exodus 27:6-7).

The altar then was to be carried by two staves or handles, which passed through four brass rings, attached to the sides of the altar. The altar is the Cross of Christ. It is to be carried throughout the whole wilderness of this world, and is to accompany us as our only hope of salvation, until we reach glory itself. The staves are two in number. The Gospel consists of two parts. One consists of the death of Christ. The other is the resurrection of the Lord Jesus Christ, and together they constitute the Gospel — the good news that:

> Christ died for our sins according to the scriptures:
> And that he was buried, and that he rose again the third day according to the scriptures (I Corinthians 15:3-4).

There were two staves or handles. One only would not have been enough, for it would not have been balanced. The two parts of the Gospel, the death, and the resurrection of Christ, balance and complement each other. The one without the other is impossible, and useless. Without the death of Christ there could, of course, have been no resurrection, and no salvation. Without the resurrection of Christ, His death was futile, fruitless, and sterile and helpless. A dead Christ can save no one — he could not save himself, but a living Christ who was dead and conquered death is a Saviour to whom all may come with absolute confidence and hope and security.

The preaching of the death of Christ, vicariously, without the resurrection is a contradiction and a deception. Without the resurrection, the Cross of Christ is an insult to our intelligence, a travesty upon God, a meaningless crime, and makes God a liar and the Bible a farce. Anything less than the declaration that Christ died, and that He arose, and that He is alive today, living in heaven, is a delusion, a snare, and a deception and a denial of the eternal Word of God. This, and this alone makes Christianity unique among all the systems of religion of the world, and sets it apart from every other philosophy of salvation. The only religion which claims a living Christ is Christianity. All the devotees of all the other religions of the world extol their leaders and point to their wonderful achievements during their lives, but they are all dead, and not even the most fanatic devotee dares to claim that their leader has risen from the dead. The resurrection of the Lord Jesus Christ is the crowning glory of the Gospel of salvation.

Its Position

In concluding this chapter we would call attention once more to the position of this altar in the tabernacle. It was not only the largest piece of furniture in the entire sanctuary but the first one in order of the seven pieces as the priest entered the tabernacle to worship. It was the starting point, the beginning of man's approach to God. Ignoring the altar barred all further progress. Avoiding the Cross makes it impossible to approach to a holy living God. We are saved, not by the life and the death of the Son of God, but by the death and the life of the Son of God.

May I repeat that statement, because it is fundamental and basic. We are not saved by Jesus' life and death, but by His death and life. His resurrection life after His death completes the Gospel story — not a perfect life of thirty-three years and then His death, and that the end of it all. That is the Devil's gospel. He would have us believe that Jesus was a perfect man, a great Teacher, a great Reformer, one whose life we should all seek to imitate and emulate. The Devil would have us to believe also that Jesus died a vicarious death for a great and noble cause, and that He is a wonderful example of martyrdom for an ideal which He cherished. All of this Satan does not object to at all; he is perfectly willing that we should believe and accept all these truths concerning Jesus Christ, just so we leave Him in the tomb, and in death. The Devil's gospel is this — that Jesus lived a wonderful life for thirty-three years, and then died a noble death, and if we are only to follow His example and imitate His virtues, all will be well with us.

But, beloved, this is not THE GOSPEL. The Gospel of the Lord Jesus Christ is this, that Christ died for our sins (not merely as our example), and that He lives today (not only that He lived a wonderful life nineteen hundred years ago). This Gospel of a crucified, risen Lord is the only Gospel worthy of the name GOOD NEWS. To be saved, therefore, one must believe all this, for:

> If thou shalt confess with thy mouth the Lord Jesus, and shalt believe in thine heart that God hath raised him from the dead, thou shalt be saved (Romans 10:9).

The sacrificial animals in the Old Testament, of course, remained in death, and were not resurrected except in type. All of this points to the inability of mere religious symbolism to bring about salvation, but confirms that it must be fulfilled in the coming of the Lord Jesus Christ, who not only died, but rose from the grave, and was:

> delivered for our offences, and was raised again for our justi·fication (Romans 4:25).

Chapter Ten

FIRE FROM HEAVEN

IN the foregoing messages we have given the general pattern of the tabernacle in detail, and have spent some time by way of introduction on the outer court, and the door of approach into the tabernacle grounds. Until we enter the door, it is impossible to behold the beauties of the interior. Until the sinner comes by way of the door of faith in God's Word, and the shed blood of the Lord Jesus, he can never behold the glories of Christ, and of His wonderful Word. The natural man is blind to the things of God. Jesus Himself said:

Except a man be born again, he cannot SEE . . . (John 3:3).

The man on the outside can see Jesus Christ as a Man, even as a perfect Man, a good Man, but he will never see Him as the Saviour and Lord until he enters the door of faith at the eastern end of the tabernacle. Just as soon as he enters, he comes face to face with the altar of burnt offering, a beautiful figure of the Cross of the Lord Jesus Christ, and he begins to realize that only by the death of another, an innocent substitute, can he be saved. On this altar he first sees an innocent animal, a substitute, its blood flowing beneath the altar, and realizes that only by the death of this substitute, and the blood of reconciliation, can he find approach unto God without judgment. The sinner will never see the gold in the tabernacle until he has seen the blood at the door of the tabernacle. The gold, we said, represents the deity of the Lord Jesus Christ. This, the natural man, through mere religion and good works and morality, cannot see until he comes by the way of the altar and the laver, the Cross and the Word of God.

NATURAL MAN BLINDED

Paul tells us in I Corinthians 2:14,

> But the natural man receiveth not the things of the Spirit of God: for they are foolishness unto him: neither can he know them, because they are spiritually discerned.

And again in II Corinthians 4:3-4, Paul gives this added light, and says:

> But if our gospel be hid, it is hid to them that are lost:
> In whom the god of this world [Satan] hath blinded the minds of them which believe not, lest the light of the glorious gospel of Christ, who is the image of God, should shine unto them.

This explains why the Bible remains to a great degree a closed book to the most educated but unconverted man, while it is an open book to the most ignorant believers. This explains why a man may be educated and trained and hold all the theological degrees that all of the theological seminaries in the world can bestow upon him, and yet be utterly blind to the great spiritual revelations of the Word of God, while a poor, uneducated believer will see truths and revelations of infinite depth and glory in this Book of Books which are absolutely indiscernible to all others. This explains why unregenerate men who have read the Bible and studied it through and through, and know the Hebrew and the Greek, will yet fail to find the virgin birth, the deity of Christ, the power of the blood, the utter depravity of man, the literal resurrection and the second coming of the Lord Jesus. "Except a man be born again he cannot *see*" these things. They are spiritually discerned. Spiritual truths are for spiritual people, and must be spiritually discerned. Therefore, without a spiritual rebirth, it is impossible for the natural man to behold these glories. At the same time, the most ignorant believer has no difficulty in finding all of these glorious truths as plain as day in the Word of God.

Until a sinner comes, therefore, by faith through Christ as Saviour and Lord, and by the Door of entrance into God's presence, he may with all his wisdom, education and culture, see no more in Jesus than just a good Man, a Teacher of great moral precepts, a noble Martyr to a noble cause, but beyond this he will not go. All of this is clearly seen in the tabernacle in the wilderness. As long as man is on the outside and refuses to come through the one door, he may look upon the white linen fence and see the human virtues and goodness of Jesus, but he will never see the gold of His deity, the glory of His Saviourhood.

THE INTERIOR BEAUTY

But when the believer enters by faith through the door, he is safe and secure, for he meets up immediately with the altar, and God's provision in the blood for all the sins of mankind. This altar of burnt offering stood just inside the door of the tabernacle. It was in the shape of a square, seven and one-half feet by seven and one-half feet, and four and one-half feet high. It was large enough to accommodate the biggest sacrificial, substitutionary animal to be sacrificed. It was built of wood, overlaid with brass. The wood speaks of the body of the Lord Jesus Christ; the brass speaks of the judgment of God upon our sins; the fire of the wrath of God which was spent upon our Saviour.

But the wood was not destroyed because it was encased in this envelope of brass. It was sealed in, air tight, by the surrounding brass; and so, even though subjected to the intense heat of the continual sacrifices which were made upon this altar, it was not consumed because oxygen (the one requirement for combustion) was hermetically excluded. What a picture of the incorruptibility of the body of the Lord Jesus Christ! Subjected to the intense heat of the wrath of God upon our sin, He was able to withstand it all, and to rise again from the dead. It was in this body that Christ bore the wrath of God for our sins. Scripture leaves no doubt about this, but tells us in I Peter 2:24 that He

bare our sins in his own body on the tree.

And Isaiah had prophesied centuries before that

the Lord hath laid on him the iniquity of us all.

But even though subjected to this intense heat of the wrath of Almighty God, He was not destroyed, but was able to say concerning His life:

No man taketh it from me, but I lay it down of myself. I have power to lay it down, and I have power to take it again (John 10:18).

The poet David, who was also a prophet, prophesied all of this one thousand years before when he said:

My flesh also shall rest in hope.

For thou wilt not leave my soul in hell; neither wilt thou suffer thine Holy One to see corruption (Psalm 16:9-10).

CONTINUAL OFFERING

The fire upon this altar was kindled from heaven. It fell from God and kindled the sacrifice on the occasion of the dedication of the tabernacle when it was completed. No human hands brought the kindling fire, no man-made fire burned upon this altar, for when the tabernacle had been completed, all the furniture in its place, the ark had been placed within the holy of holies, Moses and Aaron came out, and there was no one left in the tabernacle, and then:

There came a fire out from before the Lord, and consumed upon the altar the burnt offering and the fat: which when all the people saw, they shouted, and fell on their faces (Leviticus 9:24).

Notice carefully, that this fire fell from heaven, and was not kindled by human hands. Salvation is entirely and exclusively of the Lord (Jonah 2:9). No human effort, no human help, no human contribution was made to kindle the fire upon this altar. It must be all by the grace of God, wholly apart from all human help and merit, religion and works. To do otherwise meant certain death. The two sons of Aaron, Nadab and Abihu, in Leviticus 10, brought strange fire and were smitten by immediate death by the fire which fell upon them from heaven.

How the fire upon this altar was kindled, we do not know. Whether a bolt of lightning, or fire from the fiery pillar, or some other means was used, it came from heaven direct. This was God's method of showing His approval upon an acceptable sacrifice. In the case of Abel's sacrifice, we believe that God honored his sacrifice also by sending fire from heaven to kindle and consume the sacrifice upon the altar. In the case of Elijah, God again answered faith through fire from heaven, which fire fell upon the sacrifice on the altar and even licked up the water in the trenches about the altar. In the dedication of the temple the same thing is repeated. The lesson, of course, is evident. We are not to add anything at all to the finished work of the Lord Jesus Christ. There is nothing we can do until we have come to Calvary and received God's own finished salvation by faith in the shed blood of the Lord Jesus.

ALWAYS BURNING

This fire on the altar of burnt offering was kindled once and for all, and was never allowed to go out, and it was never to be repeated. In Leviticus 6:12, 13 we read:

> And the fire upon the altar shall be burning in it; it shall not be put out . . .
> The fire shall ever be burning upon the altar; IT SHALL NEVER GO OUT.

It was then to burn continually. It was always ready for the poor sinner who came. It was kindled by the Lord, and was never to be repeated. This, of course, speaks of the security of the believer, and the fact that the sacrifice always stands to plead for the saint who has come by way of the Cross. There is no waiting, no doubting. But there is a great deal more to the lesson of this altar of burnt offering. The fire was kindled as a perpetual testimony of the finished work of the Lord Jesus Christ. Only when the temple of Solomon was set up, and the new altar needed kindling did the fire fall again. The sacrifice of Christ is once and for all, and is never to be repeated. It suffices for all time, and all eternity. The poor sinner, once he has come by the way of the Cross, therefore, is safe forever and ever, because it is the work of God in infinite grace, and completely excludes the works and merits of man. The whole service of the altar was designed by God Himself in behalf of the sinner.

Never Sat Down

In the tabernacle the work of the priest, of course, was never done. Day after day, month after month, he needed to offer the sacrifices for the sins of the people and feed the fire upon this altar of burnt offering. But when Christ came He finished the work, and sat down at God's right hand. The Old Testament priest could never sit down in the tabernacle, for it contained not a single chair in the entire building. But when the Lord Jesus Christ our great High Priest came, He finished the work, and He made an offering once and for all. How significantly, therefore, the writer of Hebrews expounds this type, and tells us:

> For the law having a shadow of good things to come, and not the very image of the things, can never with those sacrifices which they offered year by year continually make the comers thereunto perfect.
>
> For then would they not have ceased to be offered? because that the worshipers once purged should have had no more conscience of sins.
>
> But in those sacrifices there is a remembrance again made of sins every year.
>
> For it is not possible that the blood of bulls and of goats should take away sins.
>
> And every priest standeth daily ministering and offering oftentimes the same sacrifices, which can never take away sins:
>
> But this man, after he had offered one sacrifice for sins for ever, sat down on the right hand of God;

From henceforth expecting till his enemies be made his footstool.

For by one offering he hath perfected for ever them that are sanctified (Hebrews 10:1-4, 11-14).

In concluding this message may we, therefore, press home the practical lessons which after all are the most important, for these things were written for our admonition, and for our instruction. There are two lessons that need to be learned from this message. The first is that there is only one way of approach into the presence of God, and that is to come as a poor, lost, helpless, hell-deserving sinner, to the Cross of Christ for salvation, which only can be obtained by personal faith in the Lord Jesus Christ, as represented by the door at the eastern end of the tabernacle.

The second lesson is that he is to bring absolutely nothing but the animal of sacrifice in his hands. His faith must be entirely in the shed blood of a substitute.

Nothing in my hand I bring,
Simply to Thy Cross I cling.

The final lesson is to the saint. The work of the Lord Jesus Christ upon Calvary is all-sufficient and eternal, once and for all. We are, therefore, to rest in Him, and to enter into the full and complete fellowship and service of the tabernacle, and to go on to fruitfulness and maturity in the knowledge and service of Christ.

But grow in grace, and in the knowledge of our Lord and Saviour Jesus Christ. To him be glory both now and for ever. Amen (II Peter 3:18).

Chapter Eleven

GOD'S WASH BASIN

> And the Lord spake unto Moses, saying,
>
> Thou shalt also make a laver of brass . . . to wash withal: and thou shalt put it between the tabernacle of the congregation and the altar, and thou shalt put water therein.
>
> For Aaron and his sons shall wash their hands and their feet thereat:
>
> When they go into the tabernacle of the congregation, they shall wash with water, that they die not; or when they come near to the altar to minister, to burn offering made by fire unto the Lord:
>
> So they shall wash their hands and their feet, that they die not: and it shall be a statute for ever to them, even to him and to his seed throughout their generations (Exodus 30:17-21).
>
> And he made the laver of brass, and the foot of it of brass, of the lookingglasses of the women assembling, which assembled at the door of the tabernacle of the congregation (Exodus 38:8).

AS the priest or offerer entered through the door of the tabernacle to worship Almighty God and to serve, he first came to the altar of burnt offering, picture of the death of a substitute, and the place of the blood. It pointed, as we have already mentioned in our past messages, to the Cross of the Lord Jesus Christ on Calvary, the starting point of our entire salvation. It is the place of our justification by faith, on the basis of the shed blood, and the death and resurrection of our Saviour. This settles our salvation. We are now in the tabernacle. Even though no further progress has been made, everyone who has stopped at the altar of burnt offering, and has come by faith in the Cross

of Christ is IN, and he is saved. Since Christ is the tabernacle, we are now IN CHRIST, the moment we step through
the door, and accept the sacrifice upon the altar. The priest
in the tabernacle is a type of the believer IN CHRIST.

But this is only the beginning. Salvation begins at the
Cross, but it certainly does not end there. The new-born
believer is now to go on to the next step, and then the next,
and the next, until he attains the final victory, and rests
underneath the shekinah glory in the holy of holies. And
so after the altar, he now comes next to the laver of cleansing.
This laver was a wash basin mounted on an attached ped-
estal or base, and stood in the outer court of the tabernacle.
It was made of brass, and was kept filled with clean water.
Its function was the washing of the hands and the feet of
the priests, continually, as they ministered in the tabernacle
service and worship. At the altar the priests were justified
once for all, on the basis of the shed blood; at the laver they
are now to be repeatedly cleansed from the defilement of
the world, day by day and hour by hour. The altar, therefore, speaks of justification, but the laver speaks of the
sanctifying power of the Word of the living God.

THE MATERIAL

The laver was made of solid brass, and was filled with
pure water. Brass in the Scripture, as we have already
pointed out, speaks of the judgment of God, able to withstand the fire of testing. Water is symbolic of the Word
of God. Here at the laver the "sins of the saints" are taken
care of. At the altar the "penalty" of sin was settled forever,
but at the laver the "defilement" of sins committed by the
believer after regeneration are provided for completely. The
laver speaks of separation from the world through confession
of sin, and cleansing by the Word of God. It speaks of self-
judgment, and a yielding to God for His service alone.

The laver was made from the looking glasses of the women
of Israel, which they had carried from Egypt on the Pass-

over night. Mirrors were made in those days of highly
polished brass. Now, a mirror reflects the natural features
of the individual person looking into it. Looking glasses
were for the glorification of the flesh, and the gratification
of the old nature. They are a symbol of human vanity and
human pride. The sight of a modern woman, stopping at
every window to look at herself, and taking out her mirror
from her purse to arrange her hair, powder her face, paint
her lips, even in public, is a picture of the worldly vanity
which looking glasses represent. The women of Israel were
to surrender these looking glasses, and yield them, give
them up to be made into a laver of cleansing. The laver,
then, speaks of separation from the flesh and from the world,
and from the old nature with its pride and lusts, habits and
sins.

After a person, therefore, is saved, he must next be
separated before he can go on to be of service in the tabernacle, at the table, the candlestick, and the intercessory
incense altar. This lesson has largely been forgotten in these
days of shallow, superficial gospel preaching. To make a
decision for Christ, to sign a card, to come forward in a
meeting, seems to be the end goal and purpose of salvation,
and many, many such never bear fruit as evidenced by a
change of life and a separation from the world. They continue in their old life, in their questionable business and
pursuits, and carry all the trappings and paraphernalia of
their old sinful life with them into their new-found Christian experience, and even seem to glory in their past and
sordid testimony. Except for their verbal testimony (which
we may often question), there is little other evidence of a
real vital change having been brought about in their lives.
It is much better never to give a single spoken, oral testimony, and let our life speak instead, than to be loud in
our witnessing for Christ, and then have our lives contradict
the things we claim to be.

The women gave up their looking glasses to be cast into the brazen laver in self-judgment of their sins and worldliness. The laver contained water. The water is the Word of God by which we are cleansed and sanctified. Jesus said in John 15:3,

> Now ye are clean through the word which I have spoken unto you.

In John 17:17 He prays:

> Sanctify them through thy truth: thy word is truth.

Paul says in Ephesians 5:26 concerning the Church:

> That he might sanctify and cleanse it with the washing of water by the word.

From these Scriptures and many, many more, which might be quoted, we find that the Word is the cleansing power in our lives and speaks of the water of the washing of the Word. We are not only regenerated by the washing of the water of the Word, but we are also "kept" clean by constant recourse to the Word, by confession, by a willing surrender of all those things which belong to our old nature, and by a willing submission of all to Him.

No Dimensions

The laver was the only piece of furniture in the tabernacle, the dimensions of which were not given. Minute instructions for the exact size of every other article of furniture in the building of the tabernacle were given to Moses. The size of the court, and the fence, the tabernacle, the size of the boards and the altar, and the incense altar, the table of shewbread, and the ark of the covenant, are given with minute exactitude, but not so with the laver of cleansing. There was no command as to its size or dimension. The reason is suggestive. It was limitless in its application. There was no limit to its size, or to the amount of water which it might hold.

Since the laver was for the cleansing of the priest every time he became defiled, the repeated use of the laver became necessary. God had commanded that every time the priest approached the altar or the tabernacle, he must stop and wash at the brazen laver. It must have happened a hundred times a day, over and over again, and so there is no limit to the size of the laver as given to Moses, indicating that there is an unlimited supply, and not as Peter said, "Shall I forgive my brother seven times?" but according to the pattern of the Lord, "Seventy times seven times."

No Floor in Tabernacle

The reason for all this was the absence of a floor in the tabernacle proper, and as there were no chairs, the priest could never sit down. His feet were, therefore, always on the floor. But there was no floor, except the ground, the earth upon which he walked. As a result, he became defiled every step he took, even in the service of the Lord. No chair and no floor meant that the priests feet were continually in contact with the defilement of the earth. He could not sit down and raise his feet from the floor, but in all of his service, he was in continual contact with that which speaks of defilement, and for this he needed cleansing, because the service of the Lord was an exacting service and, "they that bear the vessels of the Lord *must* be clean." Now this cleansing was accomplished by washing with the water in the laver.

This action speaks to us of the fact that while we are saved and justified, and so are IN CHRIST, we, nevertheless, are still in this world of defilement and of sin. In our business life, our social life, and even our religious life, we are constantly exposed to the defilements of the world and the flesh. The very air we breathe is polluted round about us. Many of you who read this, work with ungodly people, and have to listen to smut and filth and cursing all day long. Others are in business where competition makes it severely difficult to be honest and make a living, to compete with dishonest competitors, as is so often the case. But the Lord knew all about this, and the weaknesses of the flesh, and has made provision for our continual cleansing. There is no use denying the fact that we are in constant contact with defilement, and that we often give way to the weakness of the flesh, and we must, therefore, remember that God tells us that our only hope is, not in denying our sinfulness, but in confessing it. In I John 1:8 we read:

> If we say that we have no sin, we deceive ourselves, and the truth is not in us.

Our only recourse is the cleansing which He provides, and He has promised:

> If we CONFESS our sins, he is faithful and just to forgive us our sins, and to cleanse us from all unrighteousness (I John 1:9).

How often may we come for cleansing? The laver had no dimensions, and the quantity of water is not specified. The provision, therefore, is as boundless and limitless as the grace of God. We may come as often as we are defiled. God wants his dear children clean, and has provided a way by confession and by repentance, through the Word of God, as we have said, "not seven times, but seventy times seven." How we praise God for this limitless provision!

HANDS AND FEET

This cleansing was for the hands and for the feet. The hands speak of service; the feet of walk and of conduct. God asks of those who have been washed at the Cross from the guilt and the penalty of sin that they shall be clean in their walk and their service to Him. "They that bear the vessels of the Lord must be clean."

In conclusion we refer you to the experience of the Apostle Peter. When the Lord Jesus Christ came to Peter at the washing of the disciples' feet in John 13, the Apostle Peter objected strenuously, and demanded a complete bath at the hands of the Lord Jesus Christ. And to this our Saviour replied,

> He that is washed needeth not save to wash his feet, but is clean every whit (John 13:10).

At regeneration, the Lord reminds Peter, we are washed positionally clean, never, never, never to be repeated. Paul says in Titus,

> Not by works of righteousness which we have done, but according to his mercy he saved us, by the WASHING OF RE-GENERATION, and renewing of the Holy Ghost (Titus 3:5).

But this washed and cleansed believer still needs the washing of his feet from the defilement of sin day by day, for there is no floor in the tabernacle. As long as we are here on the earth, we are in the world, although we are not of the world, and stand in constant need of cleansing. The priest was given a complete bath upon his induction into the priesthood, on the basis of the blood. This admitted him into the tabernacle, and he is now typically forever in Christ, but in his service he still needs the constant cleansing of the laver. This the Lord Jesus Christ impressed upon Peter:

> He that is washed needeth not save to wash his feet (John 13:10).

The washing of regeneration is once for all, but, oh, believer, remember that daily we need to come to the Throne of Grace, that we may obtain mercy, and find grace to help in time of need.

In conclusion may I ask you, therefore, How much do you avail yourself of the cleansing of the laver? Are you clean before God? What is it in your life, as a believer, which robs you of your joy and your service? Will you search your heart today, and earnestly inquire as to every known and doubtful sin, and accept His cleansing, for:

> He that covereth his sins shall not prosper: but whoso confesseth and forsaketh them shall have mercy (Proverbs 28:13).

Chapter Twelve

THE FURNITURE IN GOD'S HOUSE

IN the past messages we have studied the security of the believer as represented in the tabernacle of the congregation in the wilderness. Every believer who enters the door of the tabernacle by faith in the Lord Jesus Christ comes under the blood of the burnt offering, and finds within the tabernacle a complete provision and supply for his eternal safety and security. We saw in our last message how the brazen pins, driven deeply into the desert soil, to which the cords of the tabernacle are attached, are a picture of the love of God in providing the Lord Jesus Christ who by His death and resurrection has provided eternal salvation for us. We are now ready to enter the tabernacle proper by the door on the basis of the blood, and behold the glories which He there has prepared for us.

There were exactly seven articles of furniture in the tabernacle — two in the court of the Gentiles; three in the holy place, and two in the holy of holies. Seen from the door westward, they were the altar, the laver, the table of shewbread, the golden candlestick, the altar of incense, the ark of the testimony, and over it the blood-stained mercy seat. Seven pieces of furniture—exactly seven, and no more! Seven is the number of perfection, and it speaks to us of God's perfect provision for believers who are IN CHRIST. There are seven steps from the outside, where the sinner beholds Christ merely as a man, to the inner sanctum of full and complete rest, and victory in the Lord Jesus Christ. (1) We begin with the altar, immediately after we enter the door.

The altar is a picture of the Cross. (2) Then we come to the laver of separation. This represents separation from the world and from the flesh, and from the things which defile us, through the laver of cleansing, by the washing of the water by the Word. (3) Next we approach the table of shewbread, the place of fellowship. After we have believed, and been separated, we enter the place of fellowship with other believers in the assembly, to be fed on Christ, the Bread, at the table of fellowship. (4) The fourth step is testimony, represented by the candlestick, or lampstand, fed by the oil of the Holy Spirit. We who have been saved by the blood at the altar, cleansed by the Word at the laver, drawn into fellowship at the table, fed by the Word of God, are now ready to let our light shine in testimony. As branches of the golden candlestick, we are nourished by the Holy Spirit within, to let our light shine, as Jesus said:
Ye are the light of the world (Matthew 5:14).
Let your light so shine (Matthew 5:16).
(5) Next we come to the golden incense altar—the symbol of prayer and intercession. (6) Then we enter through the veil into the most holy place, and at the ark of the covenant surrender all. (7) Sheltered under the mercy seat we find perfect peace and complete victory and rest. Seven steps: Conversion, Separation, Bible Study, Testimony, Prayer, Full Surrender, and Victory.

THE TABLE

In studying the three pieces of furniture which stood in the holy place, we take up first the table of shewbread, which stood to the north side of the holy place. It was made of acacia wood, and was overlaid with pure gold. It was three feet long, one and one-half feet wide, and two and one-fourth feet high. It had a golden crown or molding all around the outer edge to keep the twelve loaves of bread safely upon the table and to prevent them from falling upon the ground and thus being defiled. There were four golden rings, two on each side of the table, through which were passed two bars or handles made of wood and plated with gold. With these bars the table was carried from place to place by the priests whenever they were on the move.

The children of Israel were ever on the march. They were in a howling wilderness. They had no abiding place in the wilderness, and as such they are typical of the believer during this life, who passes through this world. Out of Egypt by the blood of the lamb, separated from the world, but still in the world. The tabernacle was, therefore, God's provision for their wilderness journey. They needed food. This the table and its bread provided for them in abundance. The needed guidance was provided by the golden lampstand, and they needed an intercessor and a protector, and this was found in the golden incense altar. Again we are reminded of the absolute security of the believer who abides in Christ.

The table in the tabernacle points like all the tabernacle to the Lord Jesus Christ. Both the table and the bread upon the table represent Him. On it were placed twelve loaves of bread, six each in two separate rows. The bread was flavored with frankincense. This constituted the food of the priest. About this table the priests worshiped and fellowshiped daily, on the basis of the blood of the sacrificial animal slain on the altar. The bread also speaks of the Lord Jesus Christ, the living Bread who came down from heaven. Our Saviour Himself said in John 6:35,

> I am the bread of life: he that cometh to me shall never hunger; and he that believeth on me shall never thirst.

He repeats the statement again in John 6:48 and 51,

> I am the bread of life.
> I am the living bread which came down from heaven: if any man eat of this bread, he shall live for ever.

The table, therefore, in the tabernacle pointed to the Lord Jesus, our Sustainer, and the bread on the table was symbolic of His own body. The table was the center of fellowship for the priests, the bread was the living Word, as revealed in the written Word. The lesson for us is definite and clear. We are New Testament priests, ministering unto the Lord in the Lord Jesus. We have come by way of the bloody altar, have been sanctified by the laver of the Word, and now we are to seek fellowship for worship with other saints in the holy place, which may well represent the assembling of the saints together. Every born-again believer seeks the fellowship of other saints. It is the duty of born-again believers to identify themselves with God's people in some assembly of worship with other born-again believers. That is why we urge those who are saved through these radio broadcasts, to find a Bible-believing, Bible-preaching church or assembly as soon as possible, for fellowship, worship, and for preparation for service.

The table, therefore in the holy place, speaks of fellowship; the altar of incense, of worship; the candlestick represents light for service. We are to "walk in the light, even as he is in the light." The believer cannot be independent and work alone; he needs the blessing of assembling with other believers, for "where two or three are gathered together in my name, there am I in the midst of them." It is well to remember that the Lord promises to be present "where two or three are gathered in my name." We are not to forsake the assembling of ourselves together as the custom of some is. There is not a single individual believer who has so far advanced in the things of God that he can get along without the fellowship and the blessing of saints gathering about the table of the Lord.

BASIS OF FELLOWSHIP

The basis and center of this fellowship was the table of shewbread. Around this table the priests gathered daily. Since the table and the bread are Christ, all true fellowship must be around the person and the work of the Lord

Jesus Christ. They were to feed on Him as the Bread of Life, flavored with the frankincense of the Holy Spirit. The sustaining food of the believer, then, is the Word of God, both the living Word, and the written Word, the Bible and the Holy Spirit, represented by the bread, the Word, and the frankincense, the Holy Spirit. No wonder that the most solemn and meaningful exercise of the assembly of God's people is the occasion when we gather around the table of the Lord, as members of one body, and remember His death in the breaking of the bread and the drinking of the cup.

Remember also that the bread on the table with the frankincense was the only thing placed upon the table as the food of the priests. This is all that is necessary for health and for life. There were no sauces and spices and pickles and olives and fancy salads or pie alamode; just bread. We have drifted far, far away from this simple formula today. Instead of believers coming together to fellowship around the Lord Jesus Christ, the Bread of Life, without all the extraneous paraphernalia, and just to feed on His Word, we have too often turned our services into a carnival. The Word has been pushed aside into a secondary place. Instead, we have an hour and a half of preliminaries, with singing of silly choruses and empty spirituals, and joking and laughing and horseplay. Entertainment has taken the place of worship; singing and music instead of preaching; and then a fifteen-minute sermonette, highly spiced and sensational, in order to keep people awake after all of the wearying entertainment. And then we wonder at the worldliness and the shallowness of Christians today. We have substituted or added pickles, olives, radishes, and highly seasoned extras, and have relegated the Word of Life to a side dish, which few will touch.

The assembly of the saints should be first of all a time of worship and devotion and feeding and feasting upon the Lord Jesus Christ, and not a matter of shallow entertainment. It is a sad thing indeed when a Bible-teaching service or a prayer meeting is attended by only a handful of worshipers, while a high-powered entertainer, a musical night, or moving pictures will draw packed houses. Instead of gathering around the person of Christ and feeding upon His Word, we are today regaled by cowboy stunts, ventriloquism, magic tricks, and western movies. Oh, for a return to the good old days when folks went to church not to be entertained and amused and tickled, but to worship the Lord, and to feed upon His Word, and prepare for service through the ministry of the Holy Spirit.

EAT STANDING UP

Notice further *how* the priests were to eat at this table. They must eat "standing up." There were no chairs for them to sit down. There was not a single chair in the tabernacle, for the house of God is not a place of ease and entertainment, but the place of work and service. There was work to be done, and so they ate the bread standing on their feet, ready to go about the business of serving the people. The same was true of the Passover night of Israel's deliverance from Egypt. They were to eat the Passover lamb standing, with shoes on their feet, their loins girded and with staff in hand, ready to leave for the journey on a moment's notice.

So, too, in the tabernacle; any moment the order might come to move on, and they must be ready to pick up and leave. We, too, are called upon to worship on our feet, ready to heed the call, "Come up hither." In the ordinance of the Lord's Supper, beautiful antitype of the table of shewbread, we gather in the fellowship of believers to feed upon Christ, and to wait for orders to move on. Paul says in giving the order of the Lord's Supper:

For as often as ye eat this bread, and drink this cup, ye do shew the Lord's death TILL HE COME (I Corinthians 11:26).

Christ, our living Bread, is coming back again. At any

moment the order to move may be heard from heaven. When He comes will He find us occupied with Him? Feeding upon Him? Walking in the light of the Holy Spirit? Will He find us in fellowship with Himself and with the saints of God? Will He find us feasting upon His Word, or feeding on the shallow, empty husks of formal religion? Will He find us winning souls for Him, or building a church or a denomination or defending a pet doctrine or busy in religious entertainment? Remember, one of these days the Lord of the tabernacle will come, and then we shall give an account of what we have done with Him, the Bread of Life, where we have spent our time, and how.

In conclusion, therefore, remember that the priests were to feed at this table daily. It was their daily food. We, too, are to feed upon the Bread of Life, and what it represents as our continual diet. The Bread was the result of a process of death and suffering: bread is wheat ground to powder and baked in a heated oven. It speaks of the crushing of Gethsemane, and the burning heat of Calvary. Keep that vision of the price of our salvation before your eyes, see Him groveling in the sweat and blood and tears, see Him writhing in agony on the Cross, and you will have no time for idle frivolity and empty religious entertainment and formal worship, but you will truly be found about the table of the Lord, standing on your feet, ready to serve, and ready to march on when the orders come. This we believe to be the message of the table of shewbread.

And Jesus said unto them, I am the bread of life: he that cometh to me shall never hunger; and he that believeth on me shall never thirst (John 6:35).

Chapter Thirteen

THE GOLDEN CANDLESTICK

And thou shalt make a candlestick of pure gold: of beaten work shall the candlestick be made: his shaft, and his branches, his bowls, his knops, and his flowers, shall be of the same.

And six branches shall come out of the sides of it; three branches of the candlestick out of the one side, and three branches of the candlestick out of the other side:

And thou shalt make the seven lamps thereof: and they shall light the lamps thereof, that they may give light over against it (Exodus 25:31, 32, 37).

THE candlestick was the symbol of a person. The personal pronoun is applied to it. God says that out of pure gold shall be made the candlestick, and HIS shaft and HIS branches. The personal pronoun is applied to this lamp or candlestick. The person it represents, of course, is none other than the Lord Jesus Christ, who Himself said:

I am the light of the world (John 9:5).

This golden candlestick stood on the south side of the holy place, opposite the table of shewbread with the altar of incense between. The light of the candlestick was indispensable in the service of the priests. There was no other light in the tabernacle. There were no windows provided in the pattern of the tabernacle which God showed Moses in the mount. This, to the natural man, is a mistake and an oversight, but in the plan and purpose of God it had a definite design. Not a single ray of light was allowed to come from the outside by the light of nature. The oil in the light, representing the Holy Spirit, was the only

97

source of light by which the priest was to serve in the tabernacle. The light of the candlestick points both to the Lord Jesus Christ, and also to the written Word of God, the two being inseparable. David says:

> Thy word is a lamp unto my feet, and a light unto my path (Psalm 119:105).

The believer is to walk only, therefore, by the light of the Word of God. The moment the priests wished to walk by the light of nature, they must get outside of the tabernacle, but on the outside they were unable to see the glories of the inside of the tabernacle. All the light which the sun of nature revealed was a howling wilderness, and a drab gray, unattractive building in which there was no hint of the glories which shone within. On the outside of the tabernacle, away from the light of the golden candlestick, and in the light of the sun of nature, they were excluded from the glorious vision of the Christ, as represented in the table of shewbread, the gold-plated boards, the exquisitely, artistically adorned ceiling of linen, the overspreading wings of the cherubim, and all the other glories of the interior.

The Light of Reason

The light of nature on the outside is the light of human reason, philosophy and speculation. It is a light that shuts out God in the tabernacle, and blinds the worshiper to the things which are spiritual. The light of nature is the light of human reason. Man following reason instead of faith rejects the Word of God entirely, and invents all sorts of human philosophies and theories of man's natural wisdom. He invents the theory of evolution, the innate goodness of man, the universal fatherhood of God, and the universal brotherhood of man. The light of human reason blinds the man on the outside to the vision of the altar, and the need of the precious blood of Christ. Instead of faith, he substitutes reason and philosophy. Instead of the blood as the only remedy for sin, he substitutes religion, morality, ethics, ordinances, education, psychology, and psychiatry. Paul says:

> The natural man receiveth not the things of the Spirit of God: for they are foolishness unto him: neither can he know them, because they are spiritually discerned (I Corinthians 2:14).

But the believer inside the tabernacle, which is Christ, is to walk in the light, even as He is in the light. The light of the Word of God is the only true light, the only infallible light, the only safe guide and rule of life and conduct and practice for the believer.

THE OIL

We notice next that the candlestick was fed by the oil of the sanctuary, specially ordered and prepared of God.

> And thou shalt command the children of Israel, that they bring thee pure oil olive beaten for the light, to cause the lamp to burn always (Exodus 27:20).

Oil was also used for anointing the priests. The Lord Jesus Christ is the Light of the world, and is the anointed One. The word "Messiah," translated "Christ," means literally "the anointed one." Isaiah says of Him,

> The spirit of the Lord God is upon me; because the Lord hath anointed me (Isaiah 61:1).

Peter tells us that:

> God anointed Jesus of Nazareth with the Holy Ghost and with power (Acts 10:38).

The lamp, therefore, represents the Lord Jesus Christ; the oil, the Holy Spirit. When Jesus began His ministry, the Holy Spirit came upon Him, and He went forth to defeat the Devil and Satan in the wilderness, filled with the same Holy Spirit.

THE BODY OF CHRIST

But the golden candlestick speaks not only of Christ as the Head, but also of the Church, which is His Body. The

candlestick was seven-branched — a central upright shaft with
three branches coming out of either side. The central upright shaft represents Christ as the Head of the Body,
and the six branches which came out of its side are the
members of the Body of Christ, who came out of His
wounded side, and by the blood which gushed forth are
made one with Him. We may also say that Christ represents the vine, and the six branches the Church. Jesus
said in John 15:5,

> I am the vine, ye are the branches: He that abideth in
> me, and I in him, the same bringeth forth much fruit: for
> without me ye can do nothing (John 15:5).

The one central shaft, then, represents the Lord Jesus
Christ, the Son of God, and the Head of the Church. One
is the number of deity and sovereignty. He said to Israel:

> Hear, O Israel: the Lord our God is one Lord (Deuter-
> onomy 6:4).

The Bible opens with the statement of the sovereignty
of God. "In the beginning God"! This God was Christ,
for the verse says:

> In the beginning God created the heaven and the earth
> (Genesis 1:1).

And John tells us that it was Christ Himself who was this
Creator:

> All things were made by him; and without him was not
> any thing made that was made (John 1:3).

There were six branches, however, attached to this one
central shaft. Six is the number of man. The six branches
are the men and women, the boys and the girls, united to
Christ by faith, and made one in Him. Seven branches,
but one candlestick. Seven is the number of perfection, and
all believers are by their union to Christ made perfect in
Him, nourished by the oil of the Holy Spirit, and kept
forever.

The candlestick, then, is a picture of the Church, Christ
as the Head, and we as the members, one *in* Christ, and

one *with* Christ. As the candlestick received all of its light from the oil, and not from the outside light of nature, so too the Church, the Body of Christ, is to shed forth the light of revelation, and not the light of nature. The Church, indwelt by the Holy Spirit, is to shine with the light of the Holy Spirit of God, showing forth the personality of the Lord Jesus Christ. Jesus Himself said, in Matthew 5:14,

Ye are the light of the world.

Paul said:

Ye shine as lights in the world (Philippians 2:15).

It is, then, the function of the Church to hold aloft Christ as the Light of the world, in the power of the Holy Spirit. It is not the business of the Church to meddle in politics, to enter the field of secular education, to become a school or a college of human secular knowledge. The function of the Church is not social reform, to educate in the sciences, to deal in psychology. The Church is not called to educate, train or cultivate the natural, unregenerate man. Its function is to preach the new birth, get people saved, born again, and then to train and educate and cultivate them in the worship of God and in the winning of souls. All these other matters — secular education, culture, ethics, reform, and the sciences — are good in their own places, and belong to the realm of human research and our civic and social relationships; but they are *not* the business of the Church. The true Church preaches REGENERATION; not reformation, not education, not legislation, but regeneration.

As believers we are to mingle among men in seeking all these restraining factors in society, but with the ever-conscious conviction that only regeneration can permanently answer man's dilemma of sorrow, sin and trouble. Social reforms, legislation, and moral uplift are all desirable factors in the restraining of evil in this present dispensation, and should be supported by every born-again believer, but always with the consciousness that the final answer to the sin problem and the dilemma of the world is regeneration, and the coming again of the Lord Jesus Christ. All these other things are only temporary and cannot bring a final solution.

Individual Application

The only spiritual light that men have today must come, therefore, from those who are joined and united as branches of the true candlestick to the Lord Jesus Christ. When He was here upon the earth He said:

As long as I am in the world, I am the light of the world (John 9:5).

A hymn has been written about this beautiful verse:

The whole world was lost in the darkness of sin;
The light of the world is Jesus.

But, really, this is not actually true. Jesus is not the light of the world today. If you will study the verse very carefully, you will notice that Jesus said that while He was here in the world He was the light of the world. Notice carefully, John 9:5,

As long as I am in the world, I am the light of the world.

"As long as I am in the world" — but as a visible Person in bodily form He is not here any more. He left, and went to heaven some nineteen hundred years ago, and in His human body He is not here in the world. But Jesus made provision for this, and said to His disciples before He left:

Ye are the light of the world (Matthew 5:14).

Let your light so shine before men, that they may see your good works, and glorify your Father which is in heaven (Matthew 5:16).

Our Lord Jesus Christ is gone away, and the world seeth Him no more. All the world can see is us, who are left in the world as His representatives. The only way they can see Christ is IN US and THROUGH US. Jesus said, "As long as I am in the world, I am the light of the world." But today He is in the world in the body of believers only. If men are to see Him, they must see Him IN US, or be forever shut out from His vision. We are the light of the world today.

How bright does it shine? In your job, in your social life, in your business life, can others see Jesus in you? The world has no light other than the light which we shed abroad, by holding aloft the lamp of the Word and lifting the Lord Jesus Christ and letting Him shine through us, who said:

> And I, if I be lifted up from the earth, will draw all men unto me (John 12:32).

We certainly cannot emphasize this feature of the Christian testimony enough. Christ as a visible Person, as One who walked here upon the earth nineteen hundred years ago, has gone away, and natural men cannot see Him at all. Unless we represent Him and reflect His light, they will have to remain in eternal darkness. Just as the moon reflects the light of the sun during the night when everything is dark, so too the Church of the Lord Jesus Christ today is the only light in this gathering gloom, and we are to shed forth and to reflect the light and the love of the Lord Jesus Christ. Men are far more impressed by what we are than by what we say. I believe that much of the unregenerate world today is fed up with a great deal of our modern preaching, and are waiting for a real demonstration of the love of God, and the love of Christ in our lives. Can others see Jesus in you?

Chapter Fourteen

THE PLACE OF PRAYER

And thou shalt make an altar to burn incense upon: of shittim wood shalt thou make it.

And thou shalt put it before the veil that is by the ark of the testimony, before the mercy seat that is over the testimony, where I will meet with thee.

And Aaron shall burn thereon sweet incense every morning: when he dresseth the lamps, he shall burn incense upon it.

And when Aaron lighteth the lamps at even, he shall burn incense upon it, a perpetual incense before the Lord throughout your generations.

Ye shall offer no strange incense thereon, nor burnt sacrifice, nor meat offering; neither shall ye pour drink offering thereon (Exodus 30:1, 6-9).

THESE are God's divine, heaven-sent orders for the placing of the fifth article of furniture in the tabernacle of the congregation, another one of the several types of the Lord Jesus Christ in His work of redemption. It was an altar made of wood, overlaid with pure gold. It is again a picture of the Lord Jesus in His humanity and in His deity, the wood pointing to His humanity, and the gold speaking of His unchangeable deity. It was three feet high and one and one-half feet square. It was the tallest piece of furniture in the holy place, and speaks of the highest act of worship possible, that of prayer and priestly intercession.

Its Position

It occupied the central position in the holy place, between the table of shewbread and the golden candlestick. It stood directly in front of the veil and the ark of the covenant in the holy of holies, with its covering of the bloody mercy seat. Upon it was to be offered a continual offering of incense upon coals taken from the brazen altar at the door of the tabernacle. It is the most complete type of our Saviour now in heaven as our interceding High Priest. The writer of Hebrews informs us:

> For Christ is not entered into the holy places made with hands, which are the figures of the true; but into heaven itself, now to appear in the presence of God for us (Hebrews 9:24).

The writer of Hebrews, therefore, leaves no doubt whatsoever about the typical significance of the tabernacle, as pointing to the Lord Jesus Christ. The tabernacle was in every detail a shadow and type of the coming Redeemer. He says that the holy place was a "figure of the true"; the priest was a figure of the Lord Jesus Christ; his ministry at the altar of incense a figure of Christ in heaven offering the incense of His prayers in our behalf, so that the smoke of his incense rises constantly before the ark and the mercy seat, representing the throne of God.

At the brazen altar Christ died for us, shed His blood, reconciled us to God, and made us forever secure in Him. But at the golden altar He lives in heaven to intercede for those for whom He has already died, and who are already saved. The brazen altar speaks of the death of Christ; the golden altar speaks of the living, resurrected, ascended Lord Jesus Christ. The two altars, therefore, speak of the death and the resurrection, and constitute the full message of the Gospel,

> that Christ died for our sins according to the scriptures; And that he was buried, and that he arose again the third day according to the scriptures (I Corinthians 15:3-4).

THE CONSTANT NEED

The Lord Jesus, therefore, today is in heaven offering the incense of His own intercessory work on the basis of the blood of the Cross of Calvary. Incense is a common Biblical figure for prayer and for intercession on the part of God's people. David says in Psalm 141:2,

Let my prayer be set forth before thee as incense.

The need for the priestly intercession was constant, for the priests were daily defiled by contact with the earth upon which they walked. As we have already mentioned in our previous messages, there was no floor in the tabernacle, and the priests' feet were constantly defiled by contact with the earth, and needed continuously to be washed in the brazen laver. They also needed confession and intercession at the golden altar. We today who are in Christ are also New Testament priests. We have been justified at the Cross, but we are still in a wicked world, which is no friend to grace, and we carry with us the old nature, and are constantly defiled by contact with the world and the flesh. For this we need provision, and our Lord Jesus Christ is in heaven to meet this provision and to intercede for all believers.

The golden altar is a flat denunciation of any claim to perfection in walk which the priest might make. The incense, rising before the veil was a constant reminder to the priest that he still had the old nature, that he still came short, that he still needed the intercession and the work at the altar of incense. The claim of sinless perfection, the assertion that the old nature is completely eradicated, root and branch, is a blunt denial of the priestly office and the intercessory work of the Lord Jesus Christ today at the right hand of God.

ONLY THE BLOOD

The basis of the efficacy of the golden altar lay in the blood, taken from the altar at the door of the tabernacle. Concerning the golden altar we read:

And Aaron shall make an atonement upon the horns of it once in a year WITH THE BLOOD of the sin offering of atonements (Exodus 30:10).

The intercession and the incense received their value completely and exclusively from the blood shed at the brazen altar at the entrance of the tabernacle proper. Everything rests upon the blood of the Cross, the death and the resurrection, and the shedding of the blood of Christ. Had Christ not died for us, He could not today intercede for us. The priest could not enter the holy place without blood, without first stopping at the altar of burnt offering, and making the proper sacrifice.

For Us Also

The same is true of our prayers and our intercession as well. The tabernacle not only speaks of Christ, as a Person, but also of those who are IN HIM, and have entered in by the door. And we, too, have a ministry of intercession. The highest office of the believer is intercessory prayer. Prayer is the sweetest thing that we can offer to God, more acceptable even than testimony or active service. God is more pleased with our worship than with our service, for there can be no acceptable service until we have stopped to worship first of all at the golden altar. Martha, in the home of Martha, Mary and Lazarus, served, but Mary was commended for sitting first at Jesus' feet before she served. Martha was not reproved because she served, but because she had served without first stopping to worship. The greatest privilege, therefore, which God has given to us, and the one most neglected, is the privilege of prayer and intercession, in preparation for our service for Him.

Our prayers, too, are on the basis of the shed blood of Calvary. They are heard and accepted only because of the blood. What a privilege, therefore, is ours, that we can be priests of God to pray for and to intercede for others. Think of Abraham interceding for Lot; Moses interceding for Israel, and averting the judgment of God. The work of intercession, we repeat, is the greatest privilege of the believer.

We do thank God for the thousands of you dear saints of God who intercede for us in our work of broadcasting the Gospel. Thousands of you who are sick and shut-in have complained because you were limited in your activities for service, and have bemoaned the fact that you could not be active in many other ways, as others are, and do the things others can do. But do you realize that God has given you the biggest job, and the greatest privilege of all? Many write in and say, "We cannot do much, we cannot support your program, but we do pray for you." I wonder if you who write these letters realize that praying is after all the greatest thing you can do for us. I am convinced that if it were not for you, the unseen host of unnoticed pray-ers upon your beds and in your wheel chairs, the Devil would have had the program of the Radio Bible Class off the air long ago.

How we do appreciate that little sentence so many, many of you just add at the close of your letters, "We are praying for you." You may consider it only a little thing, when you pen it, when you add to your letter the few words, "We are praying for you," but you will never know how much we appreciate and are strengthened and encouraged by this assurance, and what it has meant in assuring the continual going forth of the Gospel to the four corners of the earth. Continue to pray, beloved, for yours is a most important task.

Only For Believers

Now to return to the intercessory work of our High Priest, the Lord Jesus Christ. As the priest in the tabernacle offered incense for Israel, so we have today in heaven a great High Priest who is there to intercede for us. By the offering of the sacrifice on the brazen altar we are saved, but by the incense on the golden altar we are kept. The incense is a continual offering, by which He is able to save all those to the uttermost who come by faith to Him, seeing that He ever liveth to make intercession for us.

Here is our security then. "He ever liveth to make intercession for us." But now will you notice carefully that this intercession in heaven is ONLY FOR BELIEVERS. The priest offered incense only for those who had first of all brought their sacrifice to the brazen altar at the door of the tabernacle, and approached on the basis of shed blood. So, too, Christ in heaven today prays and intercedes only for those who have already been born again. He does NOT PRAY for sinners. The priest at the golden altar is powerless to do a single thing for the sinner, until the sinner comes first of all to the Saviour at the Cross, represented by the altar of burnt offering. The Bible leaves no doubt upon this matter. In Christ's prophetic high priestly prayer in John 17, verse 9, He says:

I pray for them: I pray NOT FOR THE WORLD, but for them which thou hast given me; for they are thine.

Jesus Christ at the right hand of God, therefore, can do absolutely nothing for the sinner, UNTIL he comes by the way of the blood and the altar and the Cross. On the Cross, the Lord Jesus did everything that God was able to do to save sinners. He exhausted Himself, in doing all that was necessary, until He was able to say, "It is finished." Now, of course, this refers to the work of redemption. The work of redemption truly was finished on the Cross of Calvary. But it did not apply to His work of intercession, for that work is still going on today, at the right hand of God. But redemption was finished. There is no more that God Almighty Himself can do for the sinner than that which He did upon the Cross of Calvary. Until the sinner receives Christ as his Saviour by faith, he cannot be saved and he cannot have Christ as His interceding High Priest. He has no intercessory Mediator until he comes first to Calvary.

I must needs go home by the way of the cross;
   There's no other way but this;
I shall ne'er get sight of the Gates of Light;
   If the way of the cross I miss.

The way of the cross leads home,
   The way of the cross leads home;
It is sweet to know, as I onward go,
   The way of the cross leads home.

Oh, sinner, do you realize that Christ cannot stand between you and God until you come first as a poor, lost, helpless undone sinner to the Cross of Calvary, and lay your hand upon the head of the sacrifice, in faith as your substitute, and receive Him in your place. Then you can enter in and feed upon the Word, and walk in the light of the golden candlestick, and be kept by the presence of our interceding Saviour on the right hand of God. But until you do, and come as a poor, lost, hell-deserving sinner and receive Christ as your personal Lord and Saviour, all of your prayers are of no avail. God never hears the prayers of sinners. Only the prayers of those who are saved are heard by the Lord Jesus Christ.

Now I recognize and realize that this statement will be challenged by many of you, but the whole point of the position of the altar of incense is that prayer is absolutely unacceptable until we have come by the way of the bloody altar of the burnt offering, which represents the Cross of Christ. Prayer without faith is absolutely worthless, and the sinner who comes to God praying without faith, accomplishes nothing. And so you may pray and pray and pray, and still go to perdition. You can chant and repeat prayers religiously, but until you receive Christ by faith, this will be of no avail. The thief on the Cross prayed too, for he said:

If thou be the Christ, save thyself and us.

He did pray for Christ to save him, but not by the way

of His death, but by coming DOWN FROM THE CROSS. He wanted Christ to avoid the death of the Cross, "to save Himself," and then he added "and us." And so we see that while he asked and prayed to be saved, he wanted to be saved not by the death of Christ but by the life of Christ. Salvation is, therefore, not being religious, not repeating prayers, not going to church, although all these things are acceptable after salvation. There is only one way to God, and that is through personal faith in the finished work and the shed blood of the Lord Jesus Christ. Abandon all of self, and rest entirely upon the work of your Substitute.

Chapter Fifteen

THE RENT VEIL

IN our journey through the tabernacle we come now to the most holy place, also called the holy of holies in Scripture. It was the innermost of the three compartments of the tabernacle. We began our journey by taking our place outside the tabernacle in the wilderness as sinners, outside of the Lord Jesus Christ. All that we were able to see from the outside was a white linen fence, speaking of the perfection of the humanity of the Lord Jesus Christ, and then the sight of the unappealing rectangular hut covered with the drab, somber, blue-grey covering of leather made from porpoise skins. This is all the unregenerate man can see in Christ. He beholds Him as the White Linen, as a good, moral, perfect man possibly, but no more. He sees Him as a despised and rejected zealot, born before His time, dying for a noble cause, a poor, helpless martyr. He may even admire Christ, but he does not *know* Him.

But then we entered the door by faith, and came face to face with the altar, and on it a bleeding, slain animal of sacrifice. It was the Cross, and there salvation became ours, and we can sing:

> I saw One hanging on a tree;
>   In agony and blood.
> He fixed His languid eyes on me,
>   As near His Cross I stood.
>
> Oh, can it be upon the Tree,
>   My Saviour died for me.
> My soul was thrilled, my heart was filled,
>   To think, He died for me.

112

After meeting the Christ of Calvary, at the altar of burnt offering, we came next to the laver of cleansing and separation by the Word of God. And now, having been saved by the blood of Christ, and separated by the Word of the living God, we are ready to enter into fellowship with other believers, as we enter into the holy place, where we see the priests assembled together for worship, representing the assembly of the saints of God, to feed upon Christ the Word, to witness for Christ the Light, and to offer the incense of our prayers in Christ's Name. So far in our journey into the tabernacle we have taken you, and we are now ready for the next and final step.

But before entering the holy of holies, we are confronted by a serious problem, for the way is barred completely by a heavy veil, or curtain, which forbids anyone to enter except the high priest once a year on the day of atonement with the precious shed blood taken from the altar of burnt offering. For him to enter at any other time meant immediate death, or to enter without blood meant death. All others, therefore, were barred, and not even the common priesthood was allowed to enter in, and any attempt to enter meant certain death. So before we can enter into the place of the ark, the veil must be taken care of, for behind this veil is the ark, the great symbol of the throne of Almighty God. But it is a throne of judgment, for a Holy God shines above the throne, and in the ark itself is that which condemns the sinner before God. In this ark reposed a copy of the broken law which God had given to Moses in the mountain, and that law speaks of judgment, condemnation and death for the sinner.

ONCE A YEAR
Only once a year, on the day of atonement, the high priest was permitted to enter, but it had to be repeated and repeated and repeated, for it was never, never accomplished and finished and done. The veil still remained, for there

could be no final putting away of sin, except by the sacrifice of Christ. The veil which barred the way to God was the body of Christ. Hebrews tells us that we can now come,

> by a new and living way, which he hath consecrated for us, THROUGH THE VEIL, THAT IS TO SAY, HIS FLESH (Hebrews 10:20).

Here we have a tremendous statement, and one which sheds a great deal of light upon the purpose of the tabernacle service. We have the New Testament interpretation of the meaning of the veil which hung between the holy place and the holy of holies. It speaks of the perfect, sinless, holy humanity of the Lord Jesus Christ. He was perfect in all things, and kept God's law in every detail. God will not and God cannot admit anyone into His presence who is not absolutely perfect, for He is holy — so holy that none but perfectly sinless ones can ever approach Him. Until we, therefore, are as holy as the Lord Jesus Christ Himself was, we cannot enter into the presence of God. The body, the sinless humanity of Christ, reminds us of what we must be if we are to be received into His presence. The veil, representing the body of Christ in his perfect humanity according to Hebrews, therefore hung between us and God as a sign, "Keep Out," and "No Admittance."

And then, "in the fulness of time Christ came, born of a woman, born under the law, to redeem them that were under the law." He veiled Himself in human flesh, and in that human body He took our sins to the Cross of Calvary, He paid the penalty, and His perfect, sinless body was broken and rent as He finished the work, and cried, "It is finished." And see what happened to the veil which represented His perfect flesh. Matthew tells us:

> Jesus, when he had cried again with a loud voice, yielded up the ghost.
>
> And, behold, the veil of the temple was rent in twain from the top to the bottom; and the earth did quake, and the rocks rent (Matthew 27:50-51).

Mark, the writer of the second Gospel, bears testimony to the same thing (Mark 15:37-38), as well as Luke (Luke 23:45).

Yes, the veil was completely rent. It was rent from the top to the bottom, not from the bottom to the top. It was not the work of man, but the work of Almighty God. The Lord Himself was satisfied with the offering which Christ made of Himself upon the Cross of Calvary, and when He cried, "It is finished," God was completely reconciled, and to prove that it was finished, God rent the veil of separation from top to bottom and opened up the way to the holy of holies for all who by faith are clothed in the righteousness of the Lord Jesus Christ.

It was a miracle. It was a heaven-sent miracle. No human hand could have done the work of rending the veil. Rabbinical writers tell us that the veil was so firmly woven that two teams of oxen pulling in opposite directions, with the veil between them, could not tear it apart. Neither could the veil be repaired, for it was rent by God's hand, from heaven. Tradition also tells us that the priests tried to mend and sew the veil together again, but were unable to, for no thread, no cord, would hold in the repaired part. It was rent once for all, and forever.

What a picture of the perfect work of reconciliation of the Lord Jesus Christ. He took our sins, the only barrier between God and man, and bore them in the body of His flesh to Calvary, and put them all away by His own precious blood, and opened the way into the very presence of God. This is the lesson of the rent veil, the way of access to God. We must of necessity read here the commentary of the Book of Hebrews on this subject.

> For there was a tabernacle made; the first, wherein was the candlestick, and the table, and the shewbread; which is called the sanctuary.
>
> And after [behind] the second veil, the tabernacle which is called the Holiest of all;

> Which had the golden censer, and the ark of the covenant overlaid round about with gold . . .
>
> Now when these things were thus ordained, the priests went always into the first tabernacle, accomplishing the service of God.
>
> But into the second went the high priest alone once every year, not without blood, which he offered for himself, and for the errors of the people:
>
> The Holy Ghost this signifying, that the way into the holiest of all was not yet made manifest, while as the first tabernacle was yet standing:
>
> Which was a figure [type] for the time then present, in which were offered both gifts and sacrifices, that could NOT make him that did the service perfect . . . (Hebrews 9:2-4, 6-9).

All this, of course, was before the advent of Calvary. But notice now as the writer of Hebrews continues:

> But Christ being come an high priest of good things to come, by a greater and more perfect tabernacle, not made with hands . . .
>
> but by his own blood he entered in once into the holy place, having obtained eternal redemption for us (Hebrews 9:11-12).

In the latter part of this same chapter, this is added:

> It was therefore necessary that the patterns of things in the heavens should be purified with these; but the heavenly things themselves with better sacrifices than these.
>
> For Christ is not entered into the holy places made with hands, which are the figures of the true; but into heaven itself, now to appear in the presence of God for us:
>
> Nor yet that he should offer himself often, as the high priest entereth into the holy place every year with blood of others . . .
>
> but now once in the end of the world [age] hath he appeared to put away sin by the sacrifice of himself (Hebrews 9:23-26).

The veil is rent, the way is open, and we now have full and free access into the very presence of God, through the rent veil of the sacrifice of the body of Christ. God now looks upon every believer IN Christ as being as perfect as

Christ Himself was. The sin question is forever settled, we are clothed in His righteousness, and we may come freely whenever we care, as often as we please, and stay as long as we wish. We are sanctified through the offering of the body of Jesus Christ once and for all. This body of the Lord Jesus Christ was represented by the veil which hung in the tabernacle between the holy place and the holy of holies, and as long as Jesus had not made the sacrifice in bearing in His own body our sins upon the tree, the way was completely barred for us to come. But through the death of Christ, and the rending and the breaking of His body, and the atonement for our sin, the way is now opened, and all of it is graphically typified in the rending of the veil at the hour of Christ's death.

Once For All

And this rending of the veil is never to be repeated; it is once for all. What security! What assurance! What comfort! Yes,

> Once for all, oh, sinner receive it.
> Once for all, oh, doubter, believe it.
> Come to the Cross, your burdens will fall,
> Christ hath redeemed us, once for all.

> Having therefore, brethren, boldness to enter into the holiest by the blood of Jesus,
> By a new and living way, which he hath consecrated for us, through the veil, that is to say, his flesh;
> And having an high priest over the house of God;
> Let us draw near with a true heart in full assurance of faith . . .
> Let us hold fast the profession of our faith without wavering; (for he is faithful that promised) (Hebrews 10:19-23).

Oh, child of God, rejoice in this, glory in this, rest in this, that He has made full provision for all your needs, and nothing has been overlooked. The new and living way to the heart of God is wide open now, once and for all. All the grief and the sorrow we bear, the doubts and fears which trouble us, are because we do not realize that the veil has been rent, the way has been opened, and the Lord is waiting, waiting for His children to rest in full and complete trust in Him. And so we would like to close with Hebrews 4:14-16:

> Seeing then that we have a great high priest, that is passed into the heavens, Jesus the Son of God, let us hold fast our profession.
>
> For we have not an high priest which cannot be touched with the feeling of our infirmities; but was in all points tempted like as we are, yet without sin.
>
> Let us therefore come boldly unto the throne of grace, that we may obtain mercy, and find grace to help in time of need.

In our next message we shall take you behind the rent veil, and stand and worship with you at the ark of the covenant, underneath the blood-sprinkled mercy seat, and should the Lord come before our next broadcast time, then it will only be an entering into the presence of Him who is foreshadowed by all these beautiful types and figures of the Old Testament. May God help us to trust Him completely and implicitly and never grieve His heart again by doubts and fears and misgivings.

Chapter Sixteen

ALONE WITH GOD

And they shall make an ark of shittim wood: two cubits and a half shall be the length thereof, and a cubit and a half the height thereof.

And thou shalt overlay it with pure gold, within and without shalt thou overlay it, and shalt make upon it a crown of gold round about.

And thou shalt put into the ark the testimony [the two tables of the law] which I shall give thee (Exodus 25:10, 11, 16).

THE ark of the covenant was the most important piece of furniture in the entire tabernacle, and becomes at the same time the most complete type and figure of the Lord Jesus Christ to be found anywhere in the Old Testament. It stood in the innermost room of the tabernacle in the most holy place. This room was a perfect cube, fifteen feet high, wide and long. It was separated from the holy place by the veil, a heavy curtain barring the entrance to the holy of holies. The ark itself was an oblong box or chest three and three-fourths feet long, two and one-fourth feet wide, and two and one-fourth feet high. It was made of wood, covered with pure gold. It again speaks in all of its detail of Christ's twofold nature, the wood standing for His perfect humanity, and the gold for His eternal deity. It speaks of Christ our ultimate safety and security for all who come to Him through the rent veil. The writer of Hebrews plainly tells us that we

might have a strong consolation, who have fled for refuge to lay hold upon the hope set before us:

Which hope we have as an anchor of the soul, both sure and stedfast, and which entereth into that WITHIN THE VEIL;

119

Whither the forerunner is for us entered, even Jesus, made an high priest for ever after the order of Melchisedec (Hebrews 6:18-20).

THREE ARKS

The ark of the covenant in the holy of holies in the tabernacle speaks of the ultimate security of the believer from judgment, a refuge from the storms of life. There are, significantly, three arks described in the Bible; namely, the ark of Noah, the ark of Moses, and the ark of the covenant. In the ark of Noah, a family of eight were kept safe and secure from judgment and brought through the flood, in which all others on the outside perished. It was sealed within and without with pitch. It was weatherproof and stormproof. No storm could harm those within the ark, for they were shut in BY God, and were shut in WITH God.

The second ark was made by Jochebed, the mother of Moses. Judgment had been decreed upon little Moses, as the sentence of death had been pronounced by Pharaoh, king of Egypt, upon all the male children of Israel, and he had commanded them to be drowned in the river Nile. But Moses was made safe in the ark of bulrushes, made by his mother, and sealed with slime and with pitch. There was security for Moses in the ark, for God was with him in the ark. Both the ark of Noah, and the ark of Moses, were made waterproof by being lined with pitch. The word for pitch in the Bible is "kaphar," and is the Old Testament word for "atonement." But atonement was always made with blood. Salvation depends upon the blood of atonement of an innocent sacrifice. Typically, then, both the ark of Noah and the ark of Moses were made safe by the application of the "typical" blood, represented by the pitch of atonement, which lined both the ark of Noah and the ark of Moses.

THE GOLDEN ARK

Both these arks were a preparation for the third ark, which was the center of the tabernacle service. It, too, was a place of shelter and refuge and safety from judgment. Within this golden ark was the law of God, which demanded the death of the sinner. It contained the law, broken by Israel, which placed them under the condemnation and the sentence of eternal death. But over this broken law, above the ark, was the mercy seat, stained with blood, and so the ark, under the blood, becomes the place of safety from judgment and becomes the symbol of security and redemption in Christ.

CHRIST OUR KING

The ark in the tabernacle wore a crown. We read in our passage:

> thou . . . shalt make upon it a crown of gold round about (Exodus 25:11b).

The ark wore a golden crown. Now as we all know, crowns are for kings to wear. They are the symbols of sovereignty and power. The ark in the tabernacle was, therefore, a type of the Lord Jesus Christ in the office of King. The Lord Jesus has three offices, that of Prophet, Priest, and King. In the court of the Gentiles, outside of the tabernacle proper, at the brazen altar, with its blood and continually burning sacrifice, we see and behold the Lord Jesus Christ as the Prophet. A prophet is one who comes from God with God's message for man. The brazen altar and the whole burnt offering point to His first coming, when He came to die on the Cross of Calvary. There He became our Prophet to redeem us, and to bring us God's message of grace.

In the holy place, however, we see Christ as our High Priest. A priest is one who intercedes for the people. In the holy place, the priest offered the incense upon the golden altar, and our Lord Jesus Christ is today in the holy place in heaven, interceding for us who have believed. But when we enter behind the veil, into the holy of holies, we meet Christ as the King, as the Sovereign, and the Absolute

Potentate, whose will and commands are absolute. This is the goal of our Christian life. We begin with Christ as prophet at the Cross, we come to Calvary, and receive Him as our Saviour, and Prophet Redeemer. Then we are to go on, and enter the holy place, feeding on the bread of Life, walking in the light of the Holy Spirit, and growing in grace by offering incense at the golden altar. This is to know Him as our present Priest in heaven, as the One who keeps us day by day through His Spirit and by His Word.

But there is still more. We are to go on to perfection (maturity), until we have crowned Him Lord of all in our hearts and in our lives, and have enthroned Him as King of all of our being. As our sovereign captain, wholly and completely surrendered to His absolute will and command, we are to acclaim Him as absolute King of our lives. How few believers have entered this experience of full surrender, of absolute yielding to Christ as King and Lord of their lives and of all that they are and possess. Too many have stopped at the altar of salvation, but never seem to go any farther. Others have entered the holy place, and are rendering service to Him, but have never completely yielded and dedicated their all to Him as Lord and absolute Master of their lives.

THREE ROOMS

The tabernacle, therefore, had three compartments, an outer court (place of sacrifice); an inner room called the holy place (place of worship); and then the innermost room or compartment, the holy of holies (place of spiritual communion with God and victory in Christ). God wants to live in a house of three rooms. When He made Adam He created him as a three-room dwelling place for Himself. Adam had a body and a soul and a spirit. This constituted the image of God in which he was created. As a tabernacle for God, he was God's dwelling place here upon the earth. But Adam sinned, and the Lord departed, because He will not dwell with sin. But when the Last Adam came, the Second Man, Christ Jesus, He became the temple of God. This temple (Jesus) again had three rooms; a body, a soul, and a spirit. He was a perfect man, and therefore was the fit tabernacle for the dwelling place of God. But He went to heaven, and since God wants to live in a house upon this earth, He now dwells in the believers individually, and the Church as the Body of Christ collectively, and He wants us to open the entire house to Him: our body, our soul, and our spirit.

God's House on Earth

Of all of this the tabernacle was a clear type and figure and shadow. First, a figure of Christ in His work of redemption; and then a picture of the believer in Christ, in the experience of salvation. The outer court of the Gentiles is typical of the body of the believer. It is the place of sacrifice. The body is always the place in which sacrifice is rendered. We are told that "Christ bore our sins in his own body on the tree." The body, represented by the outer court (the only visible part of the tabernacle), is the place of sacrifice, and Paul beseeches the Roman believers to

present [their] BODIES a living sacrifice (Romans 12:1).

As the outer, visible court represents our bodies, so the holy place is a picture of the soul of man. It is the place of worship. There one sees the priests at the table of the Lord, in the light of the golden candlestick, worshiping, interceding and praying at the incense altar. The soul is the seat of worship, the seat of our affections, our emotions, and our fellowship. Mary said when the Holy Ghost announced that she was to become the mother of the Redeemer:

My soul doth magnify the Lord.

But the place of supreme spiritual adoration is behind the veil, at the ark of the covenant, in the holy of holies, in the presence of God. It is the place of spiritual fellowship with God alone. Into this holiest of all, no two persons were ever allowed to enter at the same time. Into it, the high priest went ALONE, ALL ALONE — ALONE WITH GOD. In the holy place all of the priests assembled and worshiped together around the table of shewbread, by the light of the golden candlestick; but in the innermost sanctuary, behind the veil, personal, individual fellowship alone was permitted. This is the climax, the acme of spiritual experience and development and power in the life of the believer. The time which the high priest spent alone with God on the day of atonement, when he presented the blood, was far more important than all the days of service in the court and the worship in the holy place.

Remember, then, that the tabernacle was a house of three rooms, typically representing the threefold constitution of the believer. The outer court may be compared to the kitchen, where the needs of the body are constantly supplied. The holy place is the living room, where all the members assembled for soul worship. But the place of spiritual power is in the secret place of the Most High. We may compare it to the bedroom in the average home, the prayer room. To this we retire alone to be with God, for the highest act of worship and adoration. There we enter into spiritual experiences to be found only there and only there alone. It is the secret place of prayer, alone with God.

How much time do you spend in the secret place of communion with God? On it will depend the acceptableness of your sacrifice, and the value of your service and your worship. Most Christians spend so much time in the kitchen ministering to the body, that they have no time for personal communion with God. Many, all too many, are so busy with the fellowship in the living room that they seldom have time to enter behind the veil. Yet right there lies the power, the victory, and the reward. So busy teaching Sunday school, serving in spiritual matters, yes, even preaching, that we neglect the place of spiritual power, alone with God.

How much time do you spend alone with God? I am not asking you how much time you give to the service of the Lord, but how much time do you give to HIM? Before you began your duties of this day, Sunday, did you find time to be alone with God, to seek His guidance for this day? Or did you lay in bed until the last moment, and have to rush and hurry yourself into a fret and a stew to get breakfast, get the children ready for Sunday school, and yourself ready for church, and you found no time for communion and fellowship with the Word of God and prayer. And then you wonder why there is so little fruit; why things go wrong; why, instead of joy and peace, you are all irritated and confused when you do so much for Him.

Listen, my friend, no day begun without entering behind the veil alone with God can be a success. The measure of your spirituality is not how busy you are in church work, in religious activity, but the measure of your spirituality and power in service is determined by, "How much do you spend in the secret place behind the veil, giving to the KING the best of your time and fellowship?" I would ten thousand times rather be known as a man who had power in prayer than as one who had power in preaching, for the latter depends upon the time we spend in the first.

> Let us therefore come boldly unto the throne of grace, that we may obtain mercy, and find grace to help in time of need (Hebrews 4:16).

ERE YOU LEFT YOUR ROOM THIS MORNING, DID YOU STOP TO PRAY?

Chapter Seventeen

UNDER THE BLOOD

And thou shalt make a mercy seat of pure gold: two cubits and a half shall be the length thereof, and a cubit and a half the breadth thereof.

And thou shalt make two cherubims of gold, of beaten work shalt thou make them, in the two ends of the mercy seat.

And thou shalt put the mercy seat above upon the ark; and in the ark thou shalt put the testimony [the tables of the broken law] that I shall give thee.

And there I will meet with thee, and I will commune with thee from above the mercy seat (Exodus 25:17, 18, 21, 22).

THE ark of the testimony, a gold-plated, oblong box, stood behind the veil in the tabernacle of the congregation of Israel. It was a symbol of the throne of God, and is a picture of Christ, our Lord and King. The ark was surmounted by a crown of gold. In the ark were the tables of the law — the law which Israel had broken. The broken law demanded judgment and death for the transgressors. The law could not save; it could only condemn. It could not take away sin; it could only reveal sin. It could not give life to the sinner; it could only kill the transgressor. The law could not even spare Christ after He took our sins upon Himself and became our sin-bearer. The law killed the Lord Jesus Christ because of the sin which He bore for us. This law lay in this ark, the throne of God. The ark, therefore, by itself was a throne of judgment, condemning the sinner, demanding his death and eternal banishment from the presence of God. The veil before the ark barred the Israelite from coming to God, and the broken law threatened death to all who should dare to approach.

GOD'S PROVISION

A provision, therefore, must be made whereby sin can be removed before man can escape the condemnation of death, and the judgment of a broken law. And this the Lord marvelously and wonderfully provided in the instruction which He gave to Moses in the making of the mercy seat, to be placed over the ark, above the broken law, between it and God, who came down upon it in the shekinah pillar of holiness and fire.

THE MERCY SEAT

This mercy seat becomes, therefore, a perfect picture of the Lord Jesus Christ in His mediatorial redemptive work. He is called our "mercy seat" in Romans 3:25. Here we read concerning our Saviour:

Whom God hath set forth to be a propitiation through faith in his blood (Romans 3:25).

We point out here that the word "propitiation" is "hilasterion" in the original Greek, and means literally "mercy seat." Romans 3:25 therefore, may be freely translated, "Whom God hath set forth to be a mercy seat through faith in his blood."

This mercy seat was made of beaten gold. Christ became our mercy seat by the beating of Gethsemane and Calvary, and shed His blood to reconcile us to God by meeting the demands and the penalty of the broken law. Over this mercy seat, with out-stretched wings, stood the cherubim, symbols of the holiness of God. Without the mercy seat they would look down upon the broken law of God, and God's holiness would demand the death of the sinner. But the mercy seat was interposed between God and the broken law. Upon this mercy seat, which served actually as the cover of the ark, was sprinkled the blood from the slain

animal on the altar of burnt offering in the court of the
tabernacle. Once every year the high priest, after offering
a sacrifice for himself, and for the sins of the people, took
the blood in a basin, entered the holiest of all, behind the
veil, and sprinkled this blood upon the mercy seat, over
and above the broken law which called for the judgment
of death. And now, when God came down in the shekinah
cloud over the ark, instead of beholding the law which Israel
had broken, He saw instead the blood of atonement, and
God could not exercise the judgment of death and of the
law, for He Himself had promised:

When I see the blood, I will pass over you (Exodus 12:13).

That blood upon the mercy seat was taken from the burnt
offering, where an innocent substitute had died and shed
its atoning blood, and the penalty of the law had been met
in the substitute, and God had now been reconciled. The
ark, without the covering of blood and revealing God's holy
law, was a throne of awful judgment for Israel. By the in-
terposition of the mercy seat sprinkled with the blood of a
sacrifice, it becomes a throne of grace instead. The throne
of judgment has become a throne of grace.

ONLY IN TYPE

All of this, of course, was only a type of the work of
Him who was still to come. This sprinkling of blood on
the mercy seat was to be repeated each year by the high
priest on the day of atonement. But this blood of bulls and
of goats could not pay the price of sin; it could only atone
for the time present; it could only cover sin, but never put
it away. It must be fulfilled in the person of the Lamb of
God, and by His precious blood. All of this, therefore, was
merely a shadow of the coming One.

For the law having a shadow of good things to come, and
not the very image of the things, can never with those sacrifices which they offered year by year continually make the
comers thereunto perfect.

For then would they not have ceased to be offered? because

that the worshippers once purged should have had no more conscience of sins.

But in those sacrifices there is a remembrance again made of sins every year.

For it is not possible that the blood of bulls and of goats should take away sins.

But this man [Jesus], after he had offered one sacrifice for sins for ever, sat down on the right hand of God (Hebrews 10:1-4, 12).

The Old Testament priest was compelled to minister continually "standing on his feet." He could not sit down even for a second, for the work was never done, and so there were no chairs provided in the tabernacle at all. But when Christ said, "It is finished," He went to heaven, and "sat down." Nothing can be added to the work of Christ, neither works, ordinances, religion, education or human merit of any kind.

CHRIST IN HEAVEN

The blood was to be sprinkled, remember, on the mercy seat right after the death of the substitutionary animal of sacrifice. Now Christ is, of course, our substitute. He was slain for us upon the Cross, and entered into death for us, and when He arose, He immediately went to heaven, entered into the holy of holies in heaven, sprinkled His precious blood upon the mercy seat before the throne of God, and forever settled the sin question, and delivered us from the curse of the law.

This is clearly taught in the New Testament. Hebrews 9:12 is very definite on this:

But by his own blood he entered in once into the holy place, having obtained eternal redemption for us.

The Bible also makes plain when He accomplished this. On the morning of the resurrection He meets Mary at the tomb. As soon as Mary recognized Him, she prostrated herself before Him, and would have kissed His feet, but with shocking suddenness, Jesus emphatically says to her:

"Touch me not!"

"Touch me not"; and then He proceeds immediately to give the reason why Mary is not permitted to touch Him at all.

> For I am not yet ascended to my Father: but go to my brethren, and say unto them, I ascend unto my Father, and your Father; and to my God, and your God (John 20:17).

Literally the Lord Jesus Christ said, "Touch me not; for I now am about to ascend unto my Father."

We can understand this action when we remember that the high priest, after he had offered the sacrifice, was to enter the holy of holies, before he did anything else, with the precious blood. No one was allowed to approach him. Everyone was shut out until this was completely done. And here in the record of the meeting with Mary we have the fulfillment of this type. Here Mary meets her great High Priest, just arisen from the tomb, but before He had entered the holy of holies with the reconciling blood. And so He says to her, "Touch me not."

But that same evening Jesus appears suddenly to His disciples in the upper room, and in answer to their doubts, He now says:

> Behold my hands and my feet, that it is I myself: handle me, and see (Luke 24:39).

He says in essence, Touch Me now, and see that I am not a spirit, but man of flesh and bone. Now notice carefully that in the morning He says to Mary, "Touch me not," and the reason He gave was, "I must first ascend to finish the priestly transaction in the holy of holies." But that same night our Lord says, Now you can touch me freely; "Handle me, and see." There is, of course, no other answer except that sometime during that day, the Bible does not tell us just when, but it is evident, that He went to heaven, and in fulfillment of type presented the blood upon the mercy seat in heaven.

Oh, beloved, do you recognize the value of all of this?

It means that the work is completely done, the veil has been permanently rent, the blood has been applied, sin is not only ATONED, but God is reconciled, the law has been satisfied, and all believers have been justified forever.

Before we close, we want to leave with you a very important and practical, and we believe, comforting truth. When the high priest went into the holy of holies on the day of atonement, he needed to do nothing except to present the precious blood. The Bible does not record that the high priest ever spake a single word as he stood in the presence of God. Tradition tells us that he uttered one word, the secret, mystic name of "Javeh," but the Bible makes no mention of the priest speaking a single word. The blood was enough, for Hebrews 12:24 says that we are come

> to Jesus the mediator of the new covenant, and to the blood of sprinkling, that SPEAKETH better things than that of Abel.

The blood speaks for us. God had said, "All I need is to SEE the blood." "When I see the blood, I will pass over you." Oh, sinner, you have nothing to do but to plead the blood, for to reject the blood is to reject the Author of your salvation. And, oh, saint of God, plead the blood, for it is your key to victory over the Devil and all temptation in the world. The Devil fears the blood as he fears nothing else, and he will flee before all who claim the blood.

> And they overcame him by the blood of the Lamb, and by the word of their testimony (Revelation 12:11).

Finally, we want to sum up the teaching of the ark and the mercy seat, so that there may be no doubt left in anyone's mind. The ark by itself spoke of the judgment and the wrath of Almighty God. In it was hidden the broken law which demanded the condemnation of the sinner and the death of the transgressor. It, therefore, was a throne of judgment, and no one could approach it, for it meant death to all those who came in their own worth, and in their own merit. However, the Lord placed over this ark a covering

Chapter Eighteen

DEATH AND RESURRECTION

> Then verily the first covenant had also ordinances of divine service, and a worldly sanctuary.
>
> For there was a tabernacle made; the first, wherein was the candlestick, and the table, and the shewbread; which is called the sanctuary.
>
> And after [behind] the second veil, the tabernacle which is called the Holiest of all;
>
> Which had the golden censer, and the ark of the covenant overlaid round about with gold, wherein was the golden pot that had manna, and Aaron's rod that budded, and the tables of the covenant [the law] (Hebrews 9:1-4).

THIS tabernacle in the wilderness was minutely and detailedly patterned after a tabernacle already existing in heaven. This is made clear in Hebrews 8:

> Now of the things which we have spoken this is the sum: We have such an high priest, who is set on the right hand of the throne of the Majesty in the heavens;
>
> A minister of the sanctuary, and of the TRUE TABERNACLE, which the Lord pitched, and not man (Hebrews 8:1-2).

The tabernacle in the wilderness, erected by the children of Israel, was therefore an exact replica of this heavenly tabernacle, for Moses was strictly commanded repeatedly to follow the exact pattern shown him in the mountain.

> Moses was admonished of God when he was about to make the tabernacle: for, See, saith he, that thou make all things according to the pattern shewed to thee in the mount (Hebrews 8:5).

The heavenly tabernacle, therefore, is none other than the Lord Jesus Christ, and the tabernacle of Israel in the

133

wilderness was an exact copy of Him, in every detail from the linen fence to the ark and the mercy seat in the holy of holies. Every part of this tabernacle, in all its details, speaks of Him, and secondarily of us, who by faith are IN Him as members of His Body. By faith we are one with, and one in Christ, so that "The Christ" consists of both the head and all the members of His Body. We have already shown that every part of the tabernacle points to and is a type of Christ in some phase or aspect of His infinitely perfect person and character and work. The altar is the Cross of Christ; the laver is the Word; the candlestick, Christ the light; and so with the curtains, the colors, the table, the incense altar, and every other part.

Most Complete

But the most complete picture of the Lord Jesus in His entire redemptive work is found in the ark of the testimony. This was an oblong chest made of gold-plated wood. It stood behind the veil, and was covered by the blood-stained mercy seat. Within this ark were three different articles of tremendous significance. We read the record in Hebrews 9, and we noticed that there was a golden pot filled with manna, the food of the children of Israel in the wilderness during their long trek from Egypt to the land of Canaan. Next was placed in the ark the rod of Aaron the priest, which had budded, blossomed and yielded fruit over night, before the testimony. And then, finally, we have the two tables of the law, received by Moses on Mt. Sinai, but immediately broken by Israel while they waited for Moses to return.

Christ is the ark, as we have seen in our previous messages, and in Him we find the Bread of Life, the manna; the new resurrection life in the budding rod of Aaron; and freedom from judgment and the liberty of grace, as represented by the broken law covered by the sheltering blood upon the mercy seat. These three articles which were hidden in the ark speak of Christ's death and resurrection, and His eternal supply. The law speaks of death; the rod speaks of resurrection; and the manna speaks of Christ our sufficient supply during our wilderness journey. Together, the broken law, the budding rod, and the manna speak of the fullness of our Lord's redemption and His keeping power and security for every believer.

THE MANNA

The manna is the food of the saints. It represents Christ as our all-sufficient supply during our entire wilderness journey here upon the earth. In John 6:51 Jesus plainly says, "I am the living bread which came down from heaven." Of this person, the Lord Jesus Christ, this manna was a type, and, therefore, a golden pot full of it was carefully preserved for an eternal memorial of how God fed His people for forty years, and, therefore, becomes the promise of how Christ, the eternal Bread of Life, will keep all those who put their trust in Him, not only for this wilderness journey, but for eternity. In Exodus 16:33 we read:

> And Moses said unto Aaron, Take a pot, and put an omer full of manna therein, and lay it up before the Lord, to be kept for your generations.
> As the Lord commanded Moses, so Aaron laid it up before the Testimony, to be kept.

And that pot of manna is in existence today. It has never perished, and it has never spoiled. It is just as fresh today as the day it fell from heaven. It is a miracle of God, for the manna in the wilderness spoiled after one day, but this pot of manna has remained fresh for the past thirty-five hundred years, for it is still in existence. The ark of the covenant with its contents is in heaven today. When it was caught up from the temple into heaven, we do not know, but Revelation 11:19 tells us definitely that, when the seventh angel sounds,

> The temple of God was opened in heaven, and there was seen in his temple the ark of his testament.

The ark, therefore, according to the clear statement of the Word of God, is in heaven today, and in the ark is the inexhaustible, incorruptible supply of manna for the future food of the saints of God. The saints of the Lord will eat this manna after we get to glory. To the church of Smyrna John writes in Revelation 2:17,

> He that hath an ear, let him hear what the Spirit saith unto the churches; To him that overcometh will I give to eat of the hidden manna.

Now all of this becomes tremendously important when we remember that the manna which was supplied by God to Israel in the wilderness becomes the type and the picture of the Lord Jesus Christ, the indestructible, inexhaustible supply of the Bread of Life for every believer. He has provided for our safety for all eternity, for He said:

> And I give unto them eternal life: and they shall never perish, neither shall any man pluck them out of my hand (John 10:28).

The Budding Rod

The next thing which we find in the ark was Aaron's rod which budded. In Numbers 17 is recorded a rebellion among the children of Israel. They had objected to the priesthood being limited to the house of Aaron alone, and demanded that all of them should be allowed to minister in the tabernacle. They demanded some sort of a rotating system whereby all the tribes of Israel might have an opportunity to serve in the priestly office. This was not according to God's order, and to settle the dispute, Moses, upon the command of God, took twelve dry sticks and wrote on them the names of the twelve tribes of Israel. These twelve dry sticks he laid up before the ark of the covenant, with the understanding that the one rod which would come to life, and bud and blossom in the morning, would settle the question forever as to the tribal right of the priesthood. Twelve dry sticks laid up before the ark, and in the morning, we read:

Behold, the rod of Aaron for the house of Levi was budded, and brought forth buds, and bloomed blossoms, and yielded almonds (Numbers 17:8).

Aaron's rod became the symbol of resurrection — life out of death. After Christ was slain by the broken law, He also arose from the dead, and abides a High Priest forever after the power of an endless life. We, today, therefore, have a living Saviour, a triumphant Saviour, who conquered death and hell and sin, and therefore, is able to save to the uttermost all those who by faith come unto Him.

UNDER THE BLOOD

And all this was because of the precious blood, for over this ark with its manna, its budding rod, and its broken law, was the mercy seat with the blood sprinkled upon it on the day of atonement by the high priest. As we have already stated, that broken law demanded the death and penalty for the sinner. Until sin was paid for, Christ could not be the Bread of our eternal life. The law demanded that we remain under the sentence of death until the price was paid. And then the priest came, and with the blood of sacrifice he sprinkled the mercy seat, and it covered for all time the broken law within. God cannot see through the precious blood, for He had said, "When I see the blood, I will pass over you." The blood, therefore, is indispensable in the economy of salvation. Without the blood we remain under the sentence of death. Remove the blood from over the broken law, and judgment falls sure and fast, and the throne of God which is now a throne of grace to all who believe, becomes again a throne of judgment.

BETHSHEMESH

As a closing illustration of the indispensability of this sheltering blood, we would like to refer you to an incident recorded in I Samuel 6. The ark of the covenant had been captured by the Philistines because of the sins of Israel, but had become such a tremendous curse to these Philistines that they were driven to absolute desperation and despair, and sent the ark back, mounted on a new cart and drawn by a pair of cattle. When the ark came into the coasts · of Israel, to the city of Bethshemesh, the people rejoiced greatly at the sight of the ark, but made one terrible mistake. Moved by deep regard and concern for the ark, and probably by curiosity, whether the Philistines had disturbed or removed any of the contents, they lifted the blood-stained mercy seat from over the broken law for just a brief moment. They looked for one brief moment upon the law of God without the blood, and the judgment of God fell upon them immediately, and we have the brief, dramatic record of this tragedy in Israel in I Samuel 6:19,

> And he [God] smote the men of Beth-shemesh, BECAUSE THEY HAD LOOKED INTO THE ARK OF THE LORD, even he smote of the people fifty thousand and threescore and ten men: and the people lamented, because the Lord had smitten many of the people with a great slaughter.

You see, beloved, when we remove the blood, the throne of grace becomes a throne of judgment.

And for this reason, Israel was only kept in the favor of God by the continual application of blood of clean animals slain upon the altar continually every day, and the blood applied once every year by the high priest, and sprinkled upon the mercy seat in the presence of God. However, this could not do any more than merely atone for sin temporarily, and cover the broken law temporarily in the sight of God. It was not possible for the blood of animals to take away sin, because their blood was corruptible, but the blood of the Lord Jesus Christ, incorruptible because it was the blood of God, divine blood, precious blood, incorruptible blood, indestructible blood, was able to put away sin, and forever settle the question of our condemnation.

And so we come to the final question again, Are you under the blood?

Ah, sinner, learn the lesson. Turn from your own efforts and righteousness and take shelter under the blood of the lamb. Turn from Sinai, to Calvary. Cease your struggle to gain heaven by works, by religion, by keeping the law, and throw yourself upon the mercy and the grace of God, at the foot of the Cross, and enter into the place where you can say:

> My hope is built on nothing less,
> Than Jesus' blood and righteousness.
> I dare not trust the sweetest frame,
> But wholly lean on Jesus' Name.
>
> On Christ the solid Rock I stand;
> All other ground is sinking sand.

Chapter Nineteen

THE HOUSE OF BLOOD

> And whatsoever man there be of the house of Israel, or of
> the strangers that sojourn among you, that eateth any manner
> of blood; I will even set my face against that soul that eateth
> blood, and will cut him off from among his people.
>
> For the life of the flesh is in the blood: and I have given
> it to you upon the altar to make an atonement for your souls:
> for it is the blood that maketh an atonement for the soul.
>
> Therefore I said unto the children of Israel, No soul of
> you shall eat blood, neither shall any stranger that sojourneth
> among you eat blood (Leviticus 17:10-12).

IF there is one fact which is established beyond all controversy and contradiction, it is the sanctity of the blood in
the economy of the sacrifices of Israel. In the tabernacle in
the wilderness, God commanded that there should be only
one place of sacrifice and that was at the altar of burnt
offering which stood immediately within the door of the
tabernacle. This offering was made effective only through
the death of a substitutionary animal and the shedding of its
blood in the place and stead of the sinful children of Israel.
In order to impress upon the hearts and minds of the children of Israel the necessity of blood in making reconciliation
unto Him, God gave strict orders concerning the sanctity
of blood, even of animals. No person was allowed to eat
blood, and no person was allowed to eat any flesh or meat
from which the blood had not been thoroughly drained.

This sanctity of the blood in the tabernacle worship was
not only a legal restriction imposed upon the children of
Israel when they received the law and the testimony of

the tabernacle, but antedated this by many hundreds of years. God had already commanded Noah, immediately after his emerging from the ark, that the blood was sacred and man was not to eat any manner of blood whatsoever. After the Cross of Calvary and the resurrection of the Lord Jesus Christ, this sanctity of the blood is again established. In Chapter 15 of the Book of Acts, at the first great council in Jerusalem, the apostles re-establish the truth of the sanctity of the blood. In the instructions which the apostles gave to the Gentile believers, they again reminded them of this restriction:

> Wherefore my sentence is, that we trouble not them, which from among the Gentiles are turned to God.
> But that we write unto them, that they abstain from pollutions of idols, and from fornication, and from things strangled, and from blood (Acts 15:19-20).

This emphasis upon the sanctity of blood was not without design. It was to remind the children of Israel constantly that without the shedding of blood there could be no remission.

In the service of the tabernacle in the wilderness, which we have been studying, this was the prominent, outstanding feature of all the sacrifices. Undoubtedly the most outstanding feature of the tabernacle in the wilderness was the prominence of this blood in all of its services. It is to be found everywhere; upon the altar, the furniture, and upon the mercy seat. The foundation of the tabernacle itself speaks of blood, for it was made of silver, the money of redemption price by blood. The prominence of scarlet in the curtains of the tabernacle and the veil all speak of the necessity of blood. Everything in the entire service of the tabernacle began and ended with the shedding of the blood of sacrificial animals. At the altar of burnt offering at the entrance of the tabernacle, a continual stream of blood flowed from the thousands upon thousands of sacrificial beasts slain at the place of sacrifice, and by this blood all the rest of the service of the tabernacle was sanctified.

A HOUSE OF BLOOD

We may, therefore, appropriately call the tabernacle the House of Blood. Concerning the service of this house of blood, God commanded Moses, saying:

> And thou shalt take of the blood of the bullock, and put it upon the horns of the altar with thy finger, and pour all the blood beside the bottom of the altar (Exodus 29:12).

This same procedure was followed in the thousands of sacrifices offered on the altar.

> And thou shalt slay the ram, and thou shalt take his blood, and sprinkle it round about upon the altar (Exodus 29:16).

And the writer of Hebrews centuries later clinches the indispensable need of the blood and gives its interpretation:

> Whereupon neither the first testament was dedicated without blood.
>
> For when Moses had spoken every precept to all the people according to the law, he took the blood of calves and of goats, with water, and scarlet wool, and hyssop, and sprinkled both the book, and all the people,
>
> Saying, This is the blood of the testament which God hath enjoined unto you.
>
> Moreover he sprinkled with blood both the tabernacle, and all the vessels of the ministry.
>
> And almost all things are by the law purged with blood; and WITHOUT SHEDDING OF BLOOD IS NO REMISSION (Hebrews 9:18-22).

We see then that the tabernacle was indeed a "house of blood." But all of this blood was merely prophetic, typical, and a shadow of the blood of the coming Lamb of God. The blood of slain animals could not atone for sin. It could not take sin away. It could "cover" sin, for that is the meaning of "atonement," but it could not remove it, or reconcile man to God. The blood of animals could atone for sin, but only the blood of Christ could bring about "reconciliation" by propitiation, and so Hebrews 9:11 tells us:

> But Christ being come an high priest of good things to come, by a greater and more perfect tabernacle, not made with hands, that is to say, not of this building;
> Neither by the blood of goats and calves, BUT BY HIS OWN BLOOD he entered in once into the holy place, having obtained eternal redemption for us (Hebrews 9:11-12).

The entire service, therefore, in the tabernacle revolves around God's demand for the blood of a substitute. God is a holy God, and sin must be taken care of before reconciliation can be effected. It was God's way of emphasizing the fact that sin is an awful thing in the sight of God, and that it took the infinite price of the blood of the Son of God to take it away.

Sin had separated God and His creature, created in His own image, and there could be no reconciliation, no peace, until that which was wrong was corrected, and that which had separated man and God had been done away. Since this one thing was sin, and God's holiness absolutely prohibits Him from having anything to do with sin, this problem must be settled. The price of this atonement was blood, and the result of the atonement is that peace is restored between God and man, and reconciliation is effected.

Necessity of Atonement

And this fact brings us to the very bedrock of the plan of salvation. There are two reasons why God demanded such an awful price for man's redemption, and these two reasons are:

I. The awful holiness of God.

II. The awful sinfulness of sin.

No man can understand the atonement nor become the recipient of its salvation until he knows something of the awful holiness of God, and His terrible hatred for sin. God is first of all infinitely righteous, just and holy, so holy, in fact, that even though He is also infinite compassion, love, mercy and grace, He cannot and will not allow a single sin to go unpunished. This is basic in the plan of salvation. God is so holy, He hates sin with such a perfect hatred, that He will never permit or allow a single being in His presence without an atonement being made for all of his sin. It is a sad fact, indeed, that we hear so little in these days about the HOLINESS of God. We hear a great deal of His love and compassion, and His mercy, but very, very little of His holiness and justice and righteousness. As a result of this silence concerning God's holiness, we have formed a mean, a low, and a cheap conception of God, and fail to respect His holiness; and, therefore, we speak about the Bible and God and sacred things so lightly, joking about holy things, singing songs about Bible characters that reduce the whole revelation of God to the realm of fiction and superstition.

In the humble Christian home where I grew up, we were taught that no subject in the entire Bible should ever be used or spoken of except with the deepest reverence and awe. Never were we allowed to joke or make light of sacred things, no, not even the Devil. But how different today! We have largely lost our sense of the holiness of God, and reverence for His sacred Word. We joke and tell stories about the Bible, and Bible characters, and even about the Devil. Christians often seem to be entertained by silly jokes and references to Bible characters and fun-making preachers and singers who sense not the holiness of the things which they are handling. How regrettable that in this age there is so much of this frothy, light and irreverent handling of the holy things of God, making our services a carnival and an entertainment, rather than a place of deep reverential worship of God and the study of His Word. Even in our Christian music today we have sunk too often to the level of jungle jazz. There has recently been the introduction into many circles of a type of frothy, even silly, choruses and songs, which copy the syncopated swing and hill-billy jazz of the world, with its empty phrases repeated over and over, leaving us with no spiritual depth, but just a shallow, emotional jag. We have lost, I say, much of the reverence for holy things, because of the introduction of much of this shallow entertainment. The result of all this is that we have missed the seriousness of the holiness of God, and the terrible imprecations upon unatoned sin.

In this message it is impossible for us to go into the other feature which necessitated the atonement, the fact of sin, which is the exact opposite of the holiness of God. We shall go into this in detail in our next messages. But now we again want to emphasize the fact, before we come to the close of this message, that we are dealing with a holy God, who cannot, who will not condone sin. Every sin must be taken care of, before there can be any salvation. This, of course, puts all of us under the condemnation of death, for all of us are sinners, and therefore can never stand in God's presence without a covering for our sin. Paul tells us in Romans 3:23,

For all have sinned, and come short of the glory of God.

A provision, therefore, must be made by which this sin can be covered and finally taken away. It is impossible for man to do this by his own works, which has been proven over and over again. Especially in the history of Israel we find that only the provision of God Himself was able to take care of this terrible situation. This covering, this atonement, was provided by God, and revealed in all the Old Testament sacrifices, and pointed forward to the Lord Jesus Christ, who when He came, shed His own blood upon the Cross of Calvary, and proved and made effective that shedding by His resurrection from the dead on the third day.

We like to think of Calvary as the demonstration of the love of God for sinners. All of this is true, and we readily admit it, but behind this there is another terrible fact, and that is that the Cross of Calvary also reveals God's hatred of sin. We have a dual revelation at Calvary. First of all, we have God's terrible hatred for sin, so that He could not accept the sinner until He had demanded the death of His own precious Son. Only because of this can God's love be revealed to poor, lost humanity. The background of Calvary is judgment upon sin. The background of Calvary is the holiness of God, and His hatred of sin. To refuse God's own remedy means that we shall have to pay for our own sins throughout the endless ages of eternity. It will be terrible, therefore, for those of you who reject this offer of the precious blood, to stand before a holy God bye and bye. In the Book of Revelation we read of the rejectors of our Lord as they beheld the face of a holy God, that:

> The kings of the earth, and the great men, and rich men, and the chief captains, and the mighty men, and every bondman, and every free man, hid themselves in the dens and in the rocks of the mountains;
>
> And said to the mountains and rocks, Fall on us, and hide us from the face of him that sitteth on the throne, and from the wrath of the Lamb:
>
> For the great day of his wrath is come; and who shall be able to stand? (Revelation 6:15-17).

Oh, my friend, fall down before that holy God now, and claim the blood of reconciliation before you cry for the rocks and the mountains to fall upon you. God help you now to receive His free offer of salvation.

Chapter Twenty

THE HATRED OF GOD

IN our study of the tabernacle we have noticed again and again that the entire service of the tabernacle revolved around the shedding of blood. It began and ended with the shedding of the blood of sacrificial animals. All of this was typical and prophetic of the coming of the Lord Jesus Christ, who by His own blood was to bring about reconciliation between God and man. In Romans 5:8-11 we read:

> But God commendeth his love toward us, in that, while we were yet sinners, Christ died for us.
>
> Much more then, being now justified by his blood, we shall be saved from wrath through him.
>
> For if, when we were enemies, we were reconciled to God by the death of his Son; much more, being reconciled, we shall be saved by his life.
>
> And not only so, but we also joy in God through our Lord Jesus Christ, by whom we have now received the atonement.

I think that we should point out here, immediately, that the word "atonement," in verse 11 (the only time the word occurs in the New Testament), is really the translation of the word for "reconciliation," and it would be more proper to translate the verse: "And not only so, but we also joy in God through our Lord Jesus Christ, by whom we have now received the reconciliation."

This passage from Romans 5 is one of the great, majestic passages of the Scriptures, which sets before us in a nut-shell the fulfillment of all the tabernacle services and the shedding of the blood of all the sacrificial animals. It is the whole basis of the plan of redemption. By nature all men are the enemies of God, no matter how religious they may be. The Bible tells us that the natural man is at enmity with his Creator. In Romans 5:10 we read:

> For if, when we were enemies, we were reconciled to God by the death of his Son. . . .

The problem of the atonement, therefore, is the problem of bringing enemies together, making friends of those who by nature were separated. This could only be done by satisfying the demands of a holy God who had been outraged by man's sin, and by removing that which separated the two parties, God and man. This thing which separated man from God was sin, s-i-n. In our former message we emphasized the holiness of God as the first reason for the necessity of a blood atonement. But inseparably connected with the holiness of God is the awful fact of sin which is the exact opposite of holiness. As darkness is to light, as bitter is to sweet, as zero is to infinity, so is sin to holiness. They are an infinity apart. They represent the two poles of an infinite conflict. Because God is infinitely holy, He cannot condone the smallest sin (although there are no small sins, for all sins are great sins).

To emphasize the awfulness of sin in the sight of a holy God, we have but to go back to the first sin of the human race. You will recall the story. Adam and Eve had eaten of the fruit of the tree which God had prohibited. Now that, of course, seems in itself but a little thing. We would call it mere petty larceny, eating one fruit from a forbidden tree. In the estimate of men, and according to our moral standards, that was only a little sin. We would hardly inflict the death penalty upon an individual for taking one fruit from a tree which had been forbidden. But God did not consider it as such, for God knows nothing about "little" sins. Listen, friend, so great was that sin in the sight of God that He not only cursed man from the garden, imposed the penalty of death upon him and upon all his offspring, but God even cursed the entire creation, the earth, the birds, the animals, and every creature over which Adam was placed as the federal head. God did not wait until man had committed murder before He cursed him, but this so-called "LITTLE SIN," was the occasion for God's awful penalty and judgment. Sin is never a little thing, even though men may belittle it and call it by any other name.

The World Hates the Word "Sin"

Has it ever struck you, as it has me, that the world has tried desperately hard to rid itself of even the very mention of the word sin? It has almost entirely disappeared from the world's vocabulary. We can pick up our newspaper or magazine and read all the accounts of violence and atrocity and murder and dishonesty, but seldom are these things called "sin." Writers talk about crime and violence and death and murder and immorality, but the word SIN is carefully avoided.

Now all of this becomes very significant, for we believe it to be an attempt, consciously or unconsciously, to get rid of the idea of sin. But sin is still sin, and until there is a revival of preaching against sin in all of its awfulness, as a filthy damning rebellion against God, which it is, there cannot be a revival, but the world will continue getting worse and more rotten and more sinful than ever. By the grace of God, we, therefore, shall lift our voice against sin, not merely as a human weakness, not merely as the mistakes of a race trying to climb upward by evolutionary processes, but as that vicious, selfish, filthy thing which lies at the basis and root of all of man's troubles and trials, and which is a rebellion against a thrice-holy God, which must result in the punishment of the sinner in an eternal hell, unless it is taken care of by the blood atonement of the Son of God. That is why we preach on the subject of the blood, the only God-given remedy for sin.

Sin the Reason for Hell

Failure to realize the true, awful nature of sin lies also at the root of man's denial of eternal punishment. Man revolts at the idea that a loving God will punish His creature in an eternal hell. Modern preachers love to tell us that God is love, and that He will do no such thing at all; but all such talk is silenced immediately when we get a true picture of these two things, GOD's HOLINESS, and the AWFULNESS OF SIN. Sin is NOT a little thing. We repeat it without apology. It is the cause of every sorrow in the world. It blights lives, breaks homes, kills children, beclouds reason, slays the body, and damns the soul. See its effect in the home, the one place that was designed and patterned after the family of heaven, with Father, Son, and Holy Ghost in perfect love and accord. And yet the home has become the scene of the greatest battles in the world. In the home, because of sin, more hearts are broken, more tears are shed than anywhere else. Sin has permeated the business world. Think of the crookedness, the exploiting of the poor, the graft, the hypocrisy, the ravenous competition, the cut-throat methods, the greed of those who by the sweat and blood and toil of others amass their polluted fortunes, only that they themselves may plunge the deeper into sin. Think of what sin has done to the family of the nations. We remember the indescribable, horrible conflicts of recent memory, when the whole world of nations engaged in the most awful conflict of all history. Think of the plight of the nations today, their national bankruptcy, insecurity and division, the starving widows and orphans, the cries of the wounded and dying, the hunger and the cold and starvation, as the result of war, and we can explain it all by only one single word, s-i-n.

Even in Christendom

But see what it has done even in the realm of religion, even among those who name the name of Jesus, the Prince of Peace. Among the very ones who should be the examples of love and tolerance and forbearance, there is instead, too often confusion and chaos, with innumerable cults and sects and classes and creeds and dogmas, with fighting and bickering and condemnation of each other, and all in the name of the Lord Jesus, the Christ who prayed that we might all be one.

But let us make this thing more personal. Go with me to yonder hospital, and listen for just a moment to the cries and moans of the sick and the suffering, and you will hear just one word in the background, SIN. See the red eyes wet with tears, and think of the bleeding hearts behind those tears as they carry that loved one away. Go with me to yonder prison and see the young lives blighted and shriveled with sin, caged up like wild animals, and again we hear the whisper in the background — SIN. Follow me now to yonder asylum, and listen to the unintelligible jargon of those poor, pitiable souls with their aberated reason and deranged minds, probably because of an act committed by their grandfather when he had his fling, and the very walls seem to whisper the word, SIN, S-I-N.

But leave the confusion of the hospital and the cursing of the prison, and slip with me into the night to yonder home where lights are still lit early in the morning. See that sobbing mother as she stoops over a little crib where lies, cold and pale, that little darling, who only a little while ago was vibrant with joy, its little body throbbing and pulsating with unrestrained life. And now there it lies in the chill stillness of death. And again we hear the word in the background, SIN, for "the wages of sin is death." But, hush! Go with me now in the gloaming, and follow that man and the little flaxen-haired maiden at his side, as they silently wend their way through the sighing pines along the little gravel path among the city of the dead, until they reach a fresh little mound of earth; and there, tenderly placing a little bunch of fading flowers upon that grave, and watering them with scalding tears, they turn away to the loneliness and the bleakness of their little home, where mother's voice will never be heard again.

Ah, yes, all these experiences cry aloud one single message which cannot be forgotten: "The wages of sin is death." I challenge you to give me any other reasonable explanation for all of the misery and heartache and suffering in this old world. But the result of sin does not even end at the grave. According to the Word of God, the penalty of sin goes on into eternity because sin is a transgression, NOT only against society or an individual, but against a holy, infinitely holy God. To the sinner who dies without accepting God's atonement, God's only remedy for sin, there awaits in addition, the prospect of an eternal hell. I do not care to describe or dwell upon the awful fact of hell, and the Bible picture of the abode of the lost, except to say that Jesus, the gentle Saviour, pictures it as a place of outer darkness where the fire is never quenched and the worm never dies.

THE AWFUL PRICE OF SIN

Ah, but someone says, that preacher is altogether too dramatic in his depiction of this subject. Dramatic? Dramatic? Is not the whole history of mankind a drama? To be born, to toil, to weep, to laugh, to rejoice, to mourn, to become old, to die, what is this but a great drama of reality? But if any of you are inclined to think me too dramatic, then come with me to Calvary, and I will give you God's dramatic picture of the awfulness of sin. What does God think of sin? The answer is Calvary, for there you see the PRICE OF SIN that God demanded. Calvary is to me the most awful, the most conclusive proof of the gravity of sin. See what it took to pay the penalty. God hates sin with an indescribable hatred, and Calvary reveals not only God's love for the sinner, but back of that, His hatred for sin. It must be fully paid. And so, nineteen hundred years ago God sent into the world His Son, the Lord Jesus, to PAY FOR OUR SIN. Calvary is, therefore, more than a picture of God's love. It is a picture of sin, for without sin there would never have been a Calvary.

Born of a virgin, He laid aside His glory, walked among men preaching the holiness of God and the awfulness of sin, and then as the time for payment draws near, He gathers His little band together and tells them the meaning of His death, and leads them out into the darkness, across the brook Kidron, and into Gethsemane. And there in desperate loneliness, amidst the gnarled old olive trees of the Garden casting their sinister, ominous, eerie shadows in the light of a full Passover moon, the Son of God falls upon His face and writhes and twists in agony as "God the Father lays upon His Son the iniquity of us all." A hand reaches down from heaven holding a cup, filled to the very brim, and as the holy Saviour looks into that cup, He becomes pale with horror; His body becomes rigid with utter amazement at what He sees. His eyes stare in wild despair as the great drops of blood ooze from His unbroken skin, and finally He cries out in the agony of His soul, "My Father, if it be possible, let this cup pass from me." But the cup remains, and again the cry, and a third time He cries, "Father, if it be possible, let this cup pass from me."

WHAT WAS IN THE CUP?

What in all the world could make the Son of God shrink and cry in agony? What, oh, what was in this cup to make Him cry for deliverance? He who shrank not from the jeering mob, He who feared not those who would slay Him, He who later went without murmuring to the Cross, to die without complaint, what is this awful thing which makes Him cringe now, and cry out to the Father? Listen to me. IT WAS SIN. YOUR SIN AND MINE! The only thing Jesus ever was afraid of was sin, and so He asks the Father, "Let this cup pass from me." Must I drink that awful thing? And God seems to answer, "No, no, My Son, You do not HAVE to, but if You don't, then all the others will be lost. The only way that sinners can be saved is for You to take their sin upon Yourself, and carry it to the Cross, for sin MUST be atoned for. There is no other way."

And so with the picture of the lost world before Him, and the realization of what sin had brought about, He lifts that reeking, stench-filled cup of the world's sin, that WE might be saved. Yes, the need of the blood of atonement can be seen in the altar of the bloody tabernacle in the wilderness; but the tabernacle pointed to another scene far more dramatic, and the blood atonement can best be seen at Calvary when we realize that Almighty God could not even save His own Son from death, once He had taken our sin upon Himself.

In closing we would like to have you notice carefully one verse in Romans 8:32. It is a tremendous commentary on the righteousness of God, and the awfulness of sin:

He that SPARED NOT HIS OWN SON, but delivered him up for us all.

What a remarkable statement! Why could not God have spared His own Son? Because that Son had taken our sin upon Himself, and after God had laid upon Jesus our sin, even God the Father could not spare His own Son. How God, therefore, must hate sin, and this hatred for sin by a Holy God becomes the necessity for the atonement by blood. Sin must be punished, even though it be God's own Son, for He "became sin for us, who knew no sin." Sinner, how do you expect to escape? How do you expect God to spare you if you refuse God's atonement for sin, and insist upon standing before a holy God without having had your sin taken care of by another?

What can wash away my sin?
Nothing but the blood of Jesus.
What can make me whole again?
Nothing but the blood of Jesus.

Oh, precious is the flow,
That makes me white as snow.
No other fount I know,
Nothing but the blood of Jesus.

For it is the blood that maketh an atonement for the soul, and without shedding of blood there is no remission.

Chapter Twenty-one

RECONCILED BY BLOOD

For all have sinned, and come short of the glory of God;
Being justified freely by his grace through the redemption
that is in Christ Jesus:
  Whom God hath set forth to be a propitiation through faith
in his blood, to declare his righteousness for the remission of sins
that are past, through the forbearance of God;
  To declare, I say, at this time his righteousness: that he
might be just, and the justifier of him which believeth in
Jesus (Romans 3:23-26).

I WOULD have you notice particularly verse 25 in which
Paul tells us that Christ was "set forth to be a propitiation
through faith in his blood, to declare his righteousness for
the remission of sins that are past, through the forbearance
of God." Under the Old Testament, before the Cross of
Calvary, there was no "putting away" of sin, and no reconciliation made between God and man. There was only an
"atonement," a covering over, a passing by, and so when
the Lord Jesus Christ came He fulfilled all righteousness,
and took care of all the sins of the past, which had been
merely covered and passed over through the forbearance
of God. During the Old Testament, therefore, before the
Cross of Calvary, God typically accepted the blood of sacrificial animals slain by the thousands in the tabernacle of
the congregation, and later on in the temple, as a temporary
covering for sin, upon the promissory note that when Jesus
Christ came, He Himself, by His own precious blood, would
make full and complete reconciliation. This act of God
in the tabernacle worship, by which He passed over the

156

sins of Israel upon the basis of the blood of the slain animal, is called the "atonement."

MEANING OF THE WORD "ATONEMENT"

The Hebrew word most commonly translated "atonement" in the Old Testament and which most perfectly expresses its Biblical meaning is "kaphar," and means "to cover." The word occurs for the first time in Genesis 6:14, where we read concerning God's instructions for the building of Noah's ark:

> Make thee an ark of gopher wood; rooms shalt thou make in the ark, and shalt pitch it within and without with pitch.

It is a very interesting fact to note that the word translated "pitch" is the word for "atonement." Noah was to pitch the ark within and without with pitch. The words used are "kaphar" and "kophar," the first being the verb, and the second the noun. Literally, therefore, we can read Genesis 6:14 as, "thou shalt atone it within and without with atonement." This gives the Old Testament picture of the atonement. It means "to cover." The pitch, the "atonement," was designed to keep out the waters of judgment and to make Noah safe within. That is what the blood of the atonement in all of the Old Testament sacrifices did. It held back and restrained the judgment of God from reaching the occupants in the ark, and made them safe in spite of the fact that God was destroying the world outside.

But this blood of atonement of sacrificial offerings and beasts did not actually, and could not actually "take away" sin, for the blood of bulls and goats could not effect a reconciliation. So the blood of the atonement in the Old Testament, as shed in the tabernacle services, only held back the judgment of God until the blood of God's perfect Lamb could be shed, and then the atonement would cease, and reconciliation would result. So under the old covenant there was no full propitiation or reconciliation, but merely a covering and passing over of sin, until the time when the blood of Christ should put away sin, and man and God could be reconciled. The blood of the Old Testament atonement deferred the judgment temporarily until the coming of Christ, and then the judgment was fully paid, and for this reason the sacrifices in the tabernacle were never finished. They were to be repeated day after day and year after year.

That, too, is why the Old Testament saint was pardoned, but never justified. The word "justification" never occurs before the Cross of Calvary, and the word "pardon" never occurs after Calvary in the Bible. The blood of the animal sacrifices merely pointed to the blood of reconciliation and propitiation of the perfect sacrifice of Christ. Now then, I trust that the passage in Romans will be clear which we quoted at the beginning of this message.

> Whom God hath set forth to be a PROPITIATION through faith in his blood . . . for the remission of sins that are past, through the forbearance of God (Romans 3:25).

On the basis of the blood of the sacrifices in the tabernacle, God was able to forbear the sins of the Old Testament believer, but propitiation was not made and sins not actually "put away" until the blood of Christ was shed. This also is the reason why saints of the Old Testament could not go to heaven, but were kept in Sheol-Hades until the Cross, for until sin had been paid for, and reconciliation made, God would not permit even a pardoned sinner into His presence. The blood atonement of the Old Testament, then, merely covered sin, while the blood of Jesus took away sin and reconciled God to man.

The Need Universal

This need of atonement is not only the revelation of Scripture, but is written in the hearts of the entire human race. It is entirely consistent with the experience of human nature. Wherever man is found, even without a Bible. there is a conscience which cries for atonement. Wherever man is found, from the chill ice-bound wastes of the poles to the sweltering, torrid, steaming jungles of the tropics, man seeks after an atonement to hush that still small voice of accusation which is the heritage of all. Explorers and missionaries tell us that there is not a single tribe in the world where there is not an attempt, no matter how crude, at appeasing the gods for wrongs which man's own conscience tells him have been committed. Someone has said, "Man is incurably religious." Atheism is an invention of modern civilization; you will find no atheists among pagans and savages. Man was born with a sense of God, and a consciousness of responsibility and guilt, and those who deny the very existence of God do so more as a result of wishful thinking than genuine conviction.

But not only does the entire race believe in a God, or gods, whatever form these gods may take, whether it be a spirit, or a sacred cow, or a serpent, or a river or a mountain, there is in addition, the consciousness that this deity is angry with man, and an attempt must be made to appease this outraged god. We see it in our first parents, when, after they had sinned their eyes were opened and they knew that they were naked, and they sewed fig leaves together and made themselves aprons. It crops up again in the sacrifices of Cain and Abel, who brought their offerings unto God as an attempt at atonement for their sins. We trace it through all the bloody sacrifices of the Old Testament and the tabernacle, where countless hundreds of thousands of animals were slain, year after year, century after century, as the literal rivers of blood flowed in an unbroken stream from the court of the tabernacle and the temple. And yet all this could only avail as an atonement without any permanent benefit apart from the blood of God's one substitute, Jesus, to which all these bloody offerings pointed.

> Not all the seas of blood,
>   Which flowed until the Cross,
>   Could make a single sinner clean,
>   Or purge him from his dross.

Or, as the writer of Hebrews puts it in unmistakable language,

> For the law having a shadow of good things to come, and not the very image of the things, can never with those sacrifices which they offered year by year continually make the comers thereunto perfect.
>
> For then would they not have ceased to be offered? because that the worshippers once purged should have had no more conscience of sins.
>
> But in those sacrifices there is a remembrance again made of sins every year.
>
> For it is not possible that the blood of bulls and of goats should take away sins.
>
> Wherefore when he cometh into the world, he saith, Sacrifice and offering thou wouldest not, but a body hast thou prepared me.
>
> In burnt offerings and sacrifices for sin thou hast had no pleasure (Hebrews 10:1-6).
>
> But this man, after he had offered one sacrifice for sins for ever, sat down on the right hand of God:
>
> For by one offering he hath perfected for ever them that are sanctified (Hebrews 10:12, 14).

THE UNIVERSAL NEED

Now all of that was by revelation of God. But even without this revelation through priests and prophets, man would still have sought an atonement, for we see this search wherever man is found. We see this same conscience of sin, and the need for atonement as we watch the poor, blind, yet intensely earnest pagan father bringing his own sons and daughters to the heathen temples to offer them a fiery sacrifice upon the altar of their pagan idols. See that pagan father as he beholds his own son cast into the open fire-belching maw of the heathen fire-god, Moloch; and as he stops his ears at the cry of agony of his own flesh and blood and turns his horrified eyes from the sight of his own son burning to a crisp, it is only an expression of that irresistible yearning in the heart of man to appease an outraged deity. Behold yonder pagan mother as she tears that little suckling babe from her own warm breast, and with a cry of utter despair casts it into the river below to feed the crocodiles. Doesn't she love that baby? Ah, yes, as much as you do yours, but she is only once more yielding to that despairing conviction that the gods must be appeased for the wrongs of her life. See the ascetics as they sleep upon boards pierced with nails, eating the scantiest food, braving the cold nakedly, secluding themselves from society, and denying themselves all the pleasures of life; simply another expression of the innate, undying consciousness of sin and the need of an atonement.

But all of these fail to give peace; all have come short of the goal sought for. God's school of conscience is designed to teach men the utter futility of man's efforts to appease a holy God, and to prepare the hearts of men for the revelation of God's own plan, the Lamb of God, the Lord Jesus. And so in the fullness of time, He came not only to make atonement but to make propitiation and reconciliation for sin by His own sacrifice. We, therefore, declare that the whole plan of atonement by blood is consistent with the experience of the race and the history of mankind.

Two Basic Attributes

In the Bible God is revealed to us by His attributes, and these attributes fall into two classes — those which describe His love, and those which set forth His hatred. In the first group we have God's love, and mercy, and compassion. In the second group we have God's holiness, justice and righteousness. Now God's love yearned for and demanded the reconciliation of fallen man. After man had sinned, God's love sought and demanded his salvation. Now if God were merely perfect love, there would have been no problem at all, for He simply could have overlooked man's sin, pardoned and forgotten it, without exacting the penalty of eternal death. That is what we often do. Instead of punishing our children, love gets the best of our justice, and we just pass it by. But that was impossible with God, for in addition to His perfect love, He is also infinitely and perfectly holy, just and truthful. God had said, "In the day that thou eatest thereof thou shalt surely die." This involved more than physical death; it included spiritual death, eternal separation from God. And since God cannot lie, He must of necessity carry out the penalty. Man must die and be eternally separated from God.

But God's love is also infinite and His love demanded man's restoration into fellowship with God, while His holiness and justice demanded the eternal separation of man because of sin. And right here is the whole problem of the atonement. If God satisfies His justice and keeps His Word, man is lost forever, and God's love is left unrequited. But if He saves man without demanding the proper, eternal punishment, then God becomes a liar, for He had said, "In the day that thou eatest thereof thou shalt surely die." Someone has called this problem the "heartbreak of God." If God's love is satisfied, His justice and truth and holiness are violated. If His justice is satisfied, His love is violated. How can both of these be satisfied? Of course, there is no human solution, no human answer to this problem. It transcends all human reason and logic. But God, who in addition to infinite love and infinite justice is also infinite wisdom, found a way for the solving of this tremendous problem.

Man could not pay, for if he did, it meant eternal separation, and love demanded his restoration. It would take a man eternity to pay for his own individual sin, without his being able to pay for anyone besides himself. Angels could not do it, for God demands that man pay for man's sin.

And so God found a way, and took the responsibility upon himself. God became man, and so could take man's place, and because He was also infinite God, He could pay the infinite price for sin. And so in the fullness of time, God became Man in the person of Christ, and upon Him was placed man's guilt and sin, and He bore it to Calvary, and there suffered the agony of hell and paid the penalty of death. Because He was a man, He could substitute for man; because He was God, He could bear the infinite penalty for sin. Isaiah 53:6 tells us:

All we like sheep have gone astray; we have turned every one to his own way; and the Lord hath laid on him the iniquity of us all.

For he hath made him to be sin for us, who knew no sin; that we might be made the righteousness of God in him (II Corinthians 5:21).

And all things are of God, who hath reconciled us to himself by Jesus Christ, and hath given to us the ministry of reconciliation;

To wit, that God was in Christ, reconciling the world unto himself . . .

Now then we are ambassadors for Christ, as though God did beseech you by us: we pray you in Christ's stead, be ye reconciled to God (II Corinthians 5:18-20).

God is completely reconciled. He is perfectly satisfied with that which His Son Jesus did upon the Cross for sinners. But now you must be reconciled to God, by accepting this offer, and receiving His Son. There is no more that God or man can do, and so to refuse His offer of peace and reconciliation is to choose eternal separation instead of eternal fellowship. The sin question has been settled forever. The only sin which can now condemn you is the sin of NOT believing on the Lord Jesus Christ. There is today only one unpardonable sin, and that is the sin of refusing God's salvation. But it is not yet too late; you may still

Chapter Twenty-two

CHRIST OUR SUBSTITUTE

But Christ being come an high priest of good things to come, by a greater and more perfect tabernacle, not made with hands, that is to say, not of this building;

Neither by the blood of goats and calves, but by his own blood he entered in once into the holy place, having obtained eternal redemption for us.

For if the blood of bulls and of goats, and the ashes of an heifer sprinkling the unclean, sanctifieth to the purifying of the flesh:

How much more shall the blood of Christ, who through the eternal Spirit offered himself without spot to God, purge your conscience from dead works to serve the living God? (Hebrews 9:11-14).

IN the religious and typical ritual of the nation of Israel under the Old Testament, all worship centered and revolved about the blood of the slain animals offered in sacrifice to God. From beginning to end, from morning to night, the entire service of the tabernacle of the congregation in the wilderness revolved around the shedding of blood and the applying of blood to every portion of the worship of the nation of Israel. This was because God had laid down a principle that there could be no redemption from sin without the shedding of blood. According to the Bible, life is in the blood, and since the wages of sin is death, the only thing which can abolish death is life, and since life is in the blood, the only price for sin, the only means of restoring spiritual life, is through the shedding of the blood. But this blood must be perfect, sinless and incorruptible blood.

That is why the blood of a mere human being could not avail, since all human blood is imperfect and sinful. For the same reason the blood of animals could not avail, for the blood of animals is also corruptible blood. The only acceptable blood was the sinless blood of the Son of God. He laid aside the form of God, and took upon Him our humanity, and became a man, and in the body of that man, Christ Jesus, there flowed divine blood, sinless, incorruptible blood, and this blood was the only blood which God could or would accept as the propitiation for sins and the basis of reconciliation.

But, until that perfect blood was shed, God made provision whereby people might still be spared. The Lord instituted, under the Old Testament, the sacrifices of the typical offerings of bulls and goats and calves and heifers, and pigeons, and doves, whose blood, while it could not take away sins, could ATONE for sin. We have already seen in our past chapter that the word "atonement" means "to cover." The Old Testament sacrifices as they were presented in the tabernacle served only to "cover" man's sin. They could not, and did not put sin away or pay for it, but they postponed the penalty, passed sin over for the present, until the time when the perfect blood of Christ should serve to take sin all away. This is what Paul teaches in Romans 3:25, which we discussed in our previous chapter, and the same thing which the writer of Hebrews refers to in Hebrews 9:15.

> And for this cause he is the mediator of the new testament, that by means of death, for the redemption of the transgressions that were under the first testament, they which are called might receive the promise of eternal inheritance.

Up until the Cross, then, there could be no putting away of sin; merely a temporary covering for sin. This is again emphasized in the last part of this chapter in Hebrews, Hebrews 9:25, 26:

Nor yet that he should offer himself often, as the high
priest entereth into the holy place every year with blood of
others;
For then must he often have suffered since the foundation
of the world: but now once in the end of the world [age]
hath he appeared to PUT AWAY sin by the sacrifice of himself.

A Butcher Shop Theology

But, says someone, that is all Old Testament theology.
We have long since outgrown that bloody philosophy of
redemption in this modern age. This preaching of the blood
of a substitute is inconsistent with our modern conceptions
of the dignity of man and the love of God. Yes, I know
that our pseudo-sensitive, shallow, falsely cultivated twentieth
century theology shudders at the thought of redemption
through the blood, and the necessity of an innocent one's
dying for the sin of another. Modern preachers say, "Away
with such a preaching of salvation. We know better than
that now." We, therefore, would like to examine the facts
and see whether this is so, and whether it has any basis
in fact. I submit to you, that the teaching of substitutionary
atonement and vicarious suffering is not only Scriptural and
Biblical, but entirely in harmony with all human experience
and historical evidence. If we take one look at life in more
than a shallow, superficial way, we find that there is no
human progress without blood. All progress demands sacrifice. The price of life is death, and according to Jesus'
words, "Except a corn of wheat fall into the ground and
die, it abideth alone."

Blood in History

The now famous words of Sir Winston Churchill carry
a wealth of meaning. In discussing the price which Britain
had to pay for the defense of her liberties during the last
war, he described it as being at the expense of "blood and
sweat and tears." Sir Winston Churchill merely restated
emphatically a truth which has always been true, and was

not invented by him at all. All of history is the record of sweat and blood and tears. Take, if you will, the history of the conquest of the seas. As we relax on that mighty ocean liner that seems to be the very acme of safety and luxury, we are but to recall at what price these comforts have been purchased. Think of the thousands of lives that were sacrificed in charting the unknown seas, in the industries which were needed to build that great ship, the lives that were lost in the gradual gathering of the scientific and mechanical and meteorological knowledge and data which makes travel by ship so safe today. The very ocean is dyed a crimson hue with the blood of those who have had to lay down their lives to wrest from the sea the secrets of its whims and powers, and make it as safe as it is today.

Or read once more the history of our own fair land, America, the land of the free and the home of the brave. Were these liberties you and I enjoy today under our bill of rights purchased without blood? Ah, too well we know the record, how those early pioneers braved the cruel seas and settled in a wilderness to establish a government where liberty should prevail. The pathway of that story is strewn with the bodies of those who laid down their lives, to procure and to maintain those liberties for us. There are no blessings without sacrifice, there is no progress without blood. Or think of the rivers of blood shed by the martyrs of old as they faced the angry lions in the arena, the pillory, the fagot pile, or the human stretchers, and died for a cause and a principle, and left us a heritage of conviction and hope that is not to be measured in silver and gold.

Think of the progress of the science of medicine and surgery from the crude age of superstition and witchcraft of a few centuries ago, to our present-day, God-given methods for the relief and the cure of pain and suffering. Think of the record of the countless thousands of men and women, doctors and nurses, laboratory technicians, and willing subjects, who exposed themselves to disease and offered themselves as human guinea pigs for experiments in which they died, that we might live. They died by the hundreds in the search for a control of yellow fever, the plague, diphtheria, small pox, and other diseases, which only a generation ago decimated whole populations, and today are only a minor threat. Their history is the history of death and blood that others might live.

As you ride in your car today, think of the blood which that car cost. Think of all the men who have given their lives in the development of the auto industry. At what cost of life those sturdy metals which form the frame and motor of your car have been wrested from the bowels of the earth, the miners who died while digging the ore to make your car, that you might ride in luxury. As you ride the train, look at your ticket carefully, and you will find more than a date upon it. It is all smeared with blood, front and back, the blood of hundreds who lost their lives in the gradual development of the great railroad system which makes our land resemble a spider's web. And this price of blood applies to everything, everything, everything. To make your shoes, a calf had to die. That wool suit you have on is covered with blood, the blood of the garment worker in the woolen mill who died while making the material for your warm and comfortable suit.

The Lesson Universal

And thus we might mention every worth-while object in life. There is no blessing without sacrifice, no life without death, no progress without blood. And all this for only temporal, transient blessings and benefits. Is it, then, I ask you, unreasonable to believe that the greatest blessing of all, eternal life, should be purchased at the greatest price of all, the precious blood of the Son of God? You infidels and scoffers who despise the blood, who call us preachers, blood-mongers and ignorant, antiquated fools, you should hang your heads in shame and crawl into your holes in disgrace, for you have overlooked and ignored one of the greatest and most fundamental principles in all of nature and history; namely, that there is no progress without the shedding of blood. Shame, double shame upon you for your inexcusable ignorance! The idea of the price of blood for everything worthwhile is written in dripping, crimson letters across the mottled face of nature, and the wrinkled sheet of history, dying the ocean scarlet red as if to reflect the gorgeous sunrise of the blood atonement, while all the highways reek with blood, as if to remind us of that blood-sprinkled way that leads to God.

No, no, my friend, the Bible doctrine of the blood atonement is the most reasonable thing in the world, and in perfect harmony with all the experiences of man and the records of history.

SUBSTITUTIONARY ATONEMENT

But not only is the blood atonement consistent with the facts of nature, but it is also sufficient and substitutionary. By substitutionary we mean that Christ died for, and in the behalf and in the place of others. This, too, is in perfect harmony with experience. Christ was not a martyr who died for a principle or a cause or a conviction, but He died for sinners. He died that they might live. The Bible leaves no doubt about this. Isaiah said, "The Lord hath laid on him the iniquity of us all." And John tells us that, "He is the propitiation for our sins, and not for ours only, but for the sins of the whole world."

The world is full of human illustrations of this very truth. In large and noble letters, this story of vicarious suffering is written also on the pages of history. Dying for others is the highest expression of love we have in the world today. See the almost unthinkable tenacity of love with which a mother will watch by the crib of her babe. For days she waits upon that darling, cooling the fevered brow and ministering to its every need, the while breathing fervent prayers for its recovery. All night long, while the rest of the family is asleep, she waits and wakes and watches until the awful strain takes its toll; and while the child recovers, the mother succumbs from exhaustion and the strain to linger awhile, and then to fade and die. Follow with me now the little funeral procession which accompanies the body of this mother on her last journey, and you have an example of one who gave her life that another might live. This, my friends, is vicarious suffering, but it was to save a loved one, and only one. But think of the vicarious suffering of another, who gave His life, not for a friend, but for His enemies, gave His life that they might have life, and more than physical life, eternal life.

SUFFICIENT FOR ALL

But still more, this atonement was not only vicarious, but it was sufficient for all. The blood of Christ is sufficient to save all men. His payment for sin was complete, and He said, IT IS FINISHED. Here is where so many stumble. They argue that if the sacrifice of Christ was sufficient for all men, then all men must be saved. But we know that all men will not be saved, and so others would argue that Jesus did not die for all men, for then all would be saved. The universalist argues that all must be saved, since Christ died for all. Those who teach the doctrines of "limited" atonement say, "No, Christ died not for all men, but only for the elect." Now both of these look at the subject from a different angle. It is true, the Scripture teaches that Christ has provided salvation for all, but all will not accept it. The fact that God knew beforehand that all men would not accept, and on the basis of His foreknowledge chose only those whom He knew would believe, does not alter the fact. By the sacrifice of Christ, God is reconciled, but man, too, must be reconciled to God. God has done His part, and there is no more than this that He can do, and now He offers that completed work as a free gift to all who will believe. To those who reject, it remains as though Christ had never died.

A Closing Illustration

As an illustration of what we mean, will you imagine a man desperately ill with a terrible disease for which no remedy has been found. The sentence of death is written in his members. Now suppose that suddenly a great physician appears with an infallible remedy for this man's disease. He comes to the man, he diagnoses his case, he prepares the remedy, he offers it free to the man, although it has cost the doctor everything he possessed to produce it; yet he offers it free and without cost. But the man refuses to accept it, and turns down this gracious offer, procured at such great sacrifice and cost. What would you think of a man like that? Why, you say, the man must be crazy, he is a fool; if he dies he has no one to blame but himself. Before the doctor offered the remedy, the man was to be pitied, but now, since the remedy has been offered and he has deliberately refused, he is not to be pitied, but blamed. His blood is now upon his own head. He can blame no one but himself.

But, what of you, poor sinner, dead in trespasses and sins, and facing eternity without hope, facing the everlasting judgment of God because of your own sin, if you reject the offer of the blood of the Son of God, the only remedy for sin, and the only hope of your salvation? God freely offers it. Isaiah said:

Ho, every one that thirsteth, come ye to the waters, and he that hath no money; come ye, buy and eat (Isaiah 55:1).

And the last offer of the Bible is the offer of God's free gift:

And the Spirit and the bride say, Come. And let him that heareth say, Come. And let him that is athirst come. And whosoever will, let him take the water of life freely (Revelation 22:17).

Can anything more be said? If you wake up in a little while in eternity (and who knows how soon?), you will have none to blame but yourself if you wake up in the place of the lost. You certainly cannot blame God, for He has made ample provision. You cannot blame me, for I have tried to be faithful in presenting this offer. Come now, therefore, before it is forever too late.

> For all have sinned, and come short of the glory of God;
> Being justified FREELY by his grace through the redemption that is in Christ Jesus:
> Whom God hath set forth to be a propitiation [mercy seat] through faith in his blood (Romans 3:23-25).

HIM THAT COMETH TO ME I WILL IN NO WISE CAST OUT (John 6:37).

Chapter Twenty-three

THE SANCTITY OF BLOOD

But flesh with the life thereof, which is the blood thereof, shall ye not eat (Genesis 9:4).

THIS is part of the very first command which God gave to man after the awful judgment of the flood of Noah. After the wickedness of man had reached its peak in antediluvian days, God, in order to spare the human race from complete corruption sent a great flood upon the earth and destroyed all men except one single family which by the grace of God had still remained "perfect in his generations." With this new family on a cleansed and renewed earth, the Lord begins a new chapter in the history of humanity. No sooner had God, however, released Noah from the ark, than He gave him some instructions concerning his conduct, lest another judgment fall upon them. Chief among these instructions was the commandment, *"Eat no blood."* "But flesh with the life thereof, which is the blood thereof, shall ye not eat." Eat no blood, says God to man as he emerges on the new earth. Is there not here more than a mere suggestion that the flood may have come in part as the result of man's disregard for the "sacredness of blood"?

We know that the earth was filled with violence, and the first overt sin committed after the fall was the sin of the shedding of Abel's innocent blood. This blood cried for vengeance from the ground. If that innocent blood called for vengeance in the flood of Noah, shall God not also avenge the blood of those who today are dying because of the latter-day violence which is unquestionably in fulfillment of the words of our Lord when He said,

> And as it was in the days of Noe, so shall it be also in the days of the Son of Man (Luke 17:26).

Yes, one of these days He is coming to put an end to the reign of terror on the earth, and cleansing the world, by the judgment of the tribulation of which the flood was but a type, will bring a kingdom of peace on another renewed and cleansed earth.

Blood Is Sacred

Because life is in the blood, and not in the flesh of God's creatures, He permitted man to eat *flesh* but it must be *without blood*. God is very insistent on this point. In giving the national dietary and ceremonial laws to Israel He repeats the prohibition of Genesis 9:4.

> Moreover ye shall eat no manner of blood, whether it be of fowl or of beast, in any of your dwellings. Whatsoever soul it be that eateth any manner of blood, even that soul shall be cut off from his people (Leviticus 7:26-27).

The same injunction is repeated at greater length in Leviticus 17. God says, "It is sin to eat any manner of blood." So serious was this sin that the transgressor was to be cut off from his people. Meat which had not been thoroughly drained of its blood was unfit for food as well as all things strangled. Today, the orthodox Jew at least, still remembers this prohibition, and will eat nothing but *kosher* meat, that is, meat which is without blood and slaughtered according to the law. Every kosher meat market and every bit of kosher food is evidence of the sacredness of blood.

We Are Under Grace

Now someone will say, "But we are under grace and that command was given to the Jews under the law." That objection carries no weight. God first gave the command to Noah and Noah *was not under law.* He lived over a thousand years before the Law of Moses was given on Mt.

Sinai. More than that, after the law had been fulfilled in Christ and the age of grace ushered in, God is careful to let us know that this rule still holds, "Eat no blood." In Acts 15 we have the record of the first general church council at Jerusalem. A very vexing question had arisen in the early church after Paul and Barnabas had taken the Gospel to the Gentiles. The Jewish members of the early church insisted that these Gentile believers become circumcised and that they were to keep the law. A bitter controversy arose and a meeting was called in Jerusalem to decide this question. Paul and Barnabas came down from Antioch for the meeting, and after much disputing they were sent back to the Gentile believers at Antioch with this message,

> Forasmuch as we have heard, that certain which went out from us have troubled you with words, subverting your souls, saying, Ye must be circumcised, and KEEP THE LAW; to whom we gave no such commandment (Acts 15:24).

Please do notice carefully what the apostles said, "We gave no such commandment." They denied that they ever taught that the Church was under the law or that Gentile believers had to be circumcised. Nineteen hundred years after, the Church is still vexed by these legalists who would make Jews out of us all, but the apostles said, No, we are not under the law but under grace. The Christian does not keep the law because he *must*, but he serves God because he is so grateful for having been delivered from the law. Now notice the further instructions of the apostles:

> For it seemed good to the Holy Ghost, and to us, to lay upon you no greater burden than these necessary things; that ye abstain from meats offered to idols, and FROM BLOOD, AND FROM THINGS STRANGLED, and from fornication (Acts 15:28-29).

They were not under law, but still they were to abstain from the eating of blood, not because they were under the law, but because of the *sacredness of blood*, which is the life of all flesh. God gave the commandment to Noah one thousand years *before* the law. It held during the age of law; and after the age of the law had passed, it still holds good.

Why No Blood Now?

God's commands are never arbitrary but always logical and reasonable. Many reasons can be found for abstaining from blood. We might mention the reasons of *health* and *hygiene,* but there are two reasons which stand out most prominent.

First, the life is in the blood and *life* is sacred. It was God's special gift and the effect of His own breath. Moses tells us in Genesis, this fact:

> God formed man of the dust of the ground, and breathed into his nostrils the BREATH OF LIFE; and man became a living soul (Genesis 2:7).

Now follows closely the Biblical argument. Since life is in the blood, all flesh is lifeless without blood. Here then is Adam formed out of the dust. Just a lump of matter without life. God breathes into his nostrils and lo, he lives. Since the life is in the blood, it was *blood* which God added to that body when He breathed into him the breath of life. Adam's body was of the earth but his blood was *directly from God.* God demands that we respect that fact since it was God's own breath which filled all flesh with blood. To eat blood, therefore, is to insult the life of God, for "the life is in the blood."

The Precious Blood

There is a second and more potent reason still. The blood was God's only purchase price of redemption. When man sinned, something happened to his blood, for "life is in the blood." Instead of incorruptible and, therefore, deathless blood, Adam's blood corrupted through sin and became subject to death. To redeem this *dead* sinner, life must be again imparted. The only remedy for death is *life.* This life is in the blood, and so blood must be furnished which is sinless and incorruptible. Now none of Adam's race could do this. For in "Adam all died." "All have sinned and come short." The angels could not furnish that blood for they are spirit beings and have neither flesh nor blood. There was only one, yes, *only one*, who could furnish that blood, the virgin-born Son of God, with a human body, but sinless supernatural blood, inseminated by the Holy Ghost. This sinless, supernatural blood was the only price of redemption God could accept, without violating the integrity of His holy nature. Death can only be banished by life. A blood transfusion must be performed and provided.

BLOOD TRANSFUSION

We hear much today about blood transfusions. Many lives have been saved by this little operation. In cases of hemorrhage, and various diseases, the blood from healthy individuals is put in the veins of the suffering victim and death is cheated of its prey. Well, the greatest of all transfusions is performed when a poor sinner dead in trespasses and sins is transfused by the blood of Christ the moment he believes. The only requisite is faith in the atoning blood.

BLOOD BANKS

We hear much, too, in these days about blood banks. It is the name applied to a storehouse for blood taken from healthy individuals for future use on injured or sick persons. By adding certain preservatives to the blood taken from healthy individuals, that blood can be kept for future use in sterile containers. This preservative does not affect the potency of the blood, so that it can be used at some future date. Persons are asked to come to the hospital or laboratory to donate this blood. There this blood is taken, treated and filed away. In this way there is always an ample supply of blood for transfusion in any emergency. How wonderful the findings of science. Today, you can give your blood to save the life of some stranger a thousand miles away, a month from now.

God's Blood Bank

This is not one-millionth as wonderful as what God did nineteen centuries ago. Then there was one man who gave *all* His sinless blood on the Cross of Calvary. There a blood bank was opened and into that bank went the blood of the Lord Jesus. It suits every type, avails for everyone and is free to all who will submit to its transfusion by the Holy Spirit. All you need do is apply for it by *faith*. We must add chemicals to the blood in our blood banks to preserve it, and then it eventually deteriorates just the same, but no preservatives need be added to His precious blood, for it was *incorruptible* blood and sinless. Not one drop of that blood was lost or wasted. It is incorruptible.

> Forasmuch as ye know that ye were not redeemed with CORRUPTIBLE THINGS, as silver and gold . . . but with the precious BLOOD of Christ, as of a lamb without blemish and without spot (I Peter 1:18-19).

That blood *cannot perish*. I do not know where that blood is now; but I suspect it is in heaven somewhere just as fresh and as potent as when it was shed nineteen hundred years ago. When I get to heaven I shall not be surprised to find a diamond studded, golden basin next to the throne with the very blood, the precious incorruptible blood which was shed at Calvary, and as we gaze upon it we will sing:

> Unto him that loved us, and washed us from our sins in his own blood (Revelation 1:5).

Hallelujah for the blood! Reader, do you know that blood is as fresh today as it ever was and always will be? It cannot perish.

Oh, sinner, won't you appropriate that precious blood *now!* There is nothing else which can wash you clean from the guilt and the power of sin. Receive it today and be saved.

> If we confess our sins, he is faithful and just to forgive us our sins, and to CLEANSE us from all unrighteousness (I John 1:9).

Chapter Twenty-four

THE DAY OF ATONEMENT

> And Aaron shall bring the bullock of the sin offering, which is for himself, and shall make an atonement for himself, and for his house, and shall kill the bullock of the sin offering which is for himself (Leviticus 16:11).

AS we conclude this volume on the tabernacle of God, we feel that a few additional remarks concerning the Day of Atonement will form a fitting end to the study of the tabernacle of the congregation, the House of Blood. We recognize the fact that we have only touched the very fringe of this deep subject, and trust that this brief outline of the Day of Atonement will stimulate the reader to further study.

The Day of Atonement was the most solemn of all the sabbath days in the ritualistic, typical economy of Israel under the law. It was the sixth in order of seven annual feast days. The festive year of Israel began with the Passover feast on the fourteenth day of the first month, and was followed by the Feast of Unleavened Bread, then the First-fruits, and the Feast of Pentecost. Then after an interval of several months the last three feast days occurred toward the end of the ceremonial year. These last three feasts are called:

1. The Feast of Trumpets
2. The Day of Atonement
3. The Feast of Tabernacles.

Every one of these feast days was designed to teach in shadow and in type some aspect of the multi-sided and infinite perfection of the work of Christ in redemption. The Passover speaks of Christ on the Cross (I Corinthians 5:7). The Unleavened Bread speaks of His putting away our sins (Hebrews 9:26). The Firstfruits, of course, is a type of His resurrection (I Corinthians 15:20). The Feast of Pentecost points to the giving of the Holy Spirit (Acts 2:1). The Feast of Trumpets points to His second coming for the Church in the rapture (I Corinthians 15:52 and I Thessalonians 4:16). The Feast of Atonement speaks of the substitutionary character and the sacrificial death of the Lord Jesus Christ, while the Feast of Tabernacles points to the rest provided by Him for the people of God.

A High Day

Among these seven feasts, the most solemn and dramatic was the Feast of the Atonement. Until this very day, this is still a high day in Israel, and is called Yom Kippur. It was the busiest day of the entire year, for into it were crowded the manifold duties of the high priest, beginning with the sacrifice of a bullock upon the altar of burnt offering, and ending with the carrying away of the remainder of the carcasses without the camp.

The first thing to notice about the ritual of this day was the fact that on this day only the high priest *alone* was permitted in the tabernacle. It was the one day in the year when all the common priests were forbidden to enter, and the high priest alone entered in to make atonement. It points to our Lord Jesus Christ, who went *alone*, forsaken by men, forsaken by God, to hang for six hours upon the Cross to provide our reconciliation.

For Himself

The ritual of the Atonement began with the sacrifice of a bullock for the priest and his house. The Old Testament

priest was himself a sinner, and therefore needed a substitute for himself and a sacrifice to be slain before he could
minister in behalf of others (Leviticus 16:6; Hebrews 9:7).
Then alone was he fitted to make atonement for the people.

But how different with Christ, our Great High Priest.
He needed not first to pay for His own sin, for He was
the sinless One. He, therefore, needed to make only one
offering, not several, for the sin of others, and then He
was able to cry out, "It is finished."

MULTIPLE OFFERINGS

On the Day of Atonement the high priest sacrificed many,
many animals. First he slew a bullock and offered it for
his own sin, and the sin of his house. In conjunction with
this offering of a young bullock for a sin offering, was also
the offering of a ram for a burnt offering. Then the priest
was to take two kids of the goats for a sin offering for the
people, and for the sins of the nation, and a ram for a
sin offering.

The two goats we have discussed in an earlier chapter
in this book, and have seen in the slain goat, and the goat
abandoned in the wilderness, the story of the Gospel — the
death and the resurrection of the Lord Jesus Christ.

The next act of the priest was to take a censer full of
hot coals from the altar of burnt offering, and with sweet
incense to offer an incense offering before the veil of the
mercy seat. The next step was the very climax of the first
half of this impressive ritual. The priest is now ready to
enter into the holy of holies. He is to take of the blood
of the bullock, and entering into the most holy place, make
an atonement for his own sin first of all. He was instructed
to dip his finger in the blood taken from the altar of burnt
offering, and sprinkle it upon and before the mercy seat
seven times. All of this offering and sprinkling of blood

was to prepare the high priest to do the same thing for the people. It was only after the high priest had sacrificed the bullock and offered incense and sprinkled the blood for *his own sins,* was he ready to make an atonement for the people. And so he has to begin all over again.

REPEATED SACRIFICE

Having done all this in behalf of himself, he must now take one goat, kill it at the altar, offer its body, and sprinkle its blood upon the mercy seat seven times for the sins of the people of the nation of Israel. Then comes the final act. The high priest now takes the live goat, lays his hands upon its head, confessing over it the sins of all the people, and sends it away into the wilderness to be abandoned. And thus was concluded the solemn ritual of the Day of Atonement.

One wonders how all the events could be crowded into one single day. And then after a year the ritual had to be done all over again. Numberless were the animals slain each year, and yet the sacrifice only availed to "pass over" the sins of the people temporarily for a year at a time, and had to be repeated again and again.

But when Christ the Greater High Priest came by a better and more perfect sacrifice, He needed not first to make atonement for His own sin; all this could be eliminated. He could by one single sacrifice meet all the requirements of a holy God, and satisfy the demands of a perfect law, and say, "It is FINISHED." We repeat once more the words in Hebrews 9:6-14:

> Now when these things were thus ordained, the priests went always into the first tabernacle, accomplishing the service of God.
> But into the second went the high priest alone once every

year, not without blood, which he offered for himself, and for the errors of the people:

The Holy Ghost this signifying, that the way into the holiest of all was not yet made manifest, while as the first tabernacle was yet standing:

Which was a figure for the time then present, in which were offered both gifts and sacrifices, that could not make him that did the service perfect, as pertaining to the conscience;

Which stood only in meats and drinks, and divers washings, and carnal ordinances, imposed on them until the time of reformation.

But Christ being come an high priest of good things to come, by a greater and more perfect tabernacle, not made with hands, that is to say, not of this building;

Neither by the blood of goats and calves, but by his own blood he entered in once into the holy place, having obtained eternal redemption for us.

For if the blood of bulls and of goats, and the ashes of an heifer sprinkling the unclean, sanctifieth to the purifying of the flesh:

How much more shall the blood of Christ, who through the eternal Spirit offered himself without spot to God, purge your conscience from dead works to serve the living God?

It Is Finished

The work is done, and God Himself can do no more than that which was done by the Lord Jesus on the Cross. In concluding these messages, therefore, on the tabernacle, we want to emphasize this truth again — that God Himself knows of no other way to save a sinner than by the Cross of Calvary. Refusal to receive God's perfect provision is to choose the doom of one's own soul.

And so we conclude this series of messages on the tabernacle. We realize how fragmentary they have been and that we have only touched the fringe of the inexhaustible lessons contained in this marvelous picture of Christ. We send this volume out, however, with the prayer that it may stimulate personal study on the part of the reader to search out new and even more precious jewels from the unfathomable mine of the tabernacle of God, wonderful type and shadow of our lovely, wonderful Christ.

Now unto the King eternal, immortal, invisible, the only wise God, be honour and glory forever and ever. Amen (I Timothy 1:17).